VOL. 2

YES, GOD!

MEN'S EDITION

THE CHALLENGES.
THE COURAGE.
THE COMMITMENT.

VOL. 2

YES, GOD!

MEN'S EDITION

MICHELE NOEL-PEAKE

publish your gift

YES, GOD! VOLUME 2 MEN'S EDITION
Copyright © 2023 Michele Noel-Peake
All rights reserved.
Published by Publish Your Gift®
An imprint of Purposely Created Publishing Group, LLC

No part of this book may be reproduced, distributed or transmitted in any form by any means, graphic, electronic, or mechanical, including photocopy, recording, taping, or by any information storage or retrieval system, without permission in writing from the publisher, except in the case of reprints in the context of reviews, quotes, or references.

Scriptures marked KJV are taken from the Holy Bible, King James Version. All rights reserved.

Scriptures marked NIV are taken from the New International Version®. Copyright © 1973, 1978, 1984, 2011 by Biblica, Inc.™. All rights reserved.

Scriptures marked NKJV are taken from the New King James Version®. Copyright © 1982 by Thomas Nelson. All rights reserved.

Scriptures marked NLT are taken from the New Living Translation®. Copyright © 1996, 2004, 2007, 2013 by Tyndale House Foundation. All rights reserved.

Scriptures marked ESV are taken from English Standard Version®. Copyright © 2001 by Crossway, a publishing ministry of Good News Publishers. All rights reserved.

Scriptures marked NLV are taken from the New Life Version, copyright © 1969 and 2003. Used by permission of Barbour Publishing, Inc., Uhrichsville, Ohio 44683. All rights reserved.

Scriptures marked NASB1995 are taken from the New American Standard Bible®. Copyright © 1960, 1962, 1963, 1968, 1971, 1972, 1973, 1975, 1977, 1995 by The Lockman Foundation. Used by permission.

Printed in the United States of America
ISBN: 978-1-64484-614-8
ISBN: 978-1-64484-615-5

Special discounts are available on bulk quantity purchases by book clubs, associations and special interest groups. For details email: sales@publishyourgift.com or call (888) 949-6228.

For information log on to www.PublishYourGift.com

Table of Contents

Foreword vii
Acknowledgements xi
Introduction 1

It Was Good That I Was Afflicted
Dominique Clark 5

God Chaser
Anthony Proctor 17

He Saved Me Before He Saved Me
Harold Ferrell 29

How God Used Me and Kept Me Through the Loss and Grief of My Wife
Grayling V.G. Sterling Sr. 41

Yes, And…
Andre Reynolds 53

You Can Build a Relationship with God Right Where You Are!
Troy Burgess 67

God Opened a Door for Me
Rodney Peake 79

About the Authors 93

Foreword

But God! There was a time in my life when I lost everything. But God! I didn't know if I would ever regain anything I lost, including my dignity, my pride, or something I wanted very much, to get married again. But God!

I have learned that children are visual, and as a child, I watched my mother work most of the time to provide the best for our family. That is what I thought was a good recipe for success. Therefore, when I got married, I worked three jobs to provide for my family. However, I was never there for my family. In my spare time, I was hanging out, I didn't communicate with my wife, I didn't cultivate the marriage, and I didn't nurture the marriage. One day, I came home from my second job, and the house was empty. My ex-wife had packed the house and the children and was gone. I didn't know where she and the kids had moved to or how to contact them. At that moment, I realized I had a failed marriage. But God!

After losing my marriage, I went into a downward spiral. I started hanging out more often because I didn't have any family to go home to. I also started drinking more and using drugs. One morning, my doorbell rang, and when I opened the door, it was the sheriff, police, and moving company. They had come to put me out of the house and to put a padlock on my door. I was immediately evicted, and my home was foreclosed on. Soon after that, the two cars that I owned were repossessed. Now here I am, sitting on my front steps with nowhere to live and no transportation to get to work. But God!

With no other options, I ended up living with my ex-wife's sister. That ended up being temporary because her daughter came back home to live, which meant they didn't have any room for me. Thank God my niece was moving and had three months left on her lease, so she let me take over the remaining months of the lease. Around that time, I had to file for bankruptcy, and in the process of doing that, my job went bankrupt and closed down. Now, I had no job and only a month to go on the lease. I realized that after that, I would have nowhere to live. Time was going into the last ten days of the last month on the lease, and things didn't look good. I had no job, no car (I was taking public transportation), in ten days, no place to live, and I was still caught up in drinking and drugs. But God!

Being in the position that I was in, I didn't know what else to do, but the one thing I could think of to do…go to God! Having been raised in the church (even though I wasn't saved), I remembered the things my mother had taught me. I got down on my knees and prayed to God. I asked Him to deliver me from drinking and drugs and to help me find a job and a place to live. How many of you know that God will provide, and not only will He provide, but he will restore because he is a God of provision and restoration? What God did next was beyond anything that I could ever ask or imagine. God took me totally out of the city I was living in, away from the drinking and drugs and away from the bad influences and living environment. And miraculously, He completely took the taste of drugs and drinking out of my mouth. God gave me a job paying double what I was previously making, plus a fully furnished apartment in a high-rise, with a company car to travel back and forth to work. Not only that, but God also restored my credit to the point that I was able to purchase items that I needed. See, God not only gives you everything you need, but if you pray and ask Him, he will give you everything you want.

Not long after, God brought a woman back into my life, who had been a friend of mine for over twenty years, and joined us together spiritually. We ended up getting married, starting a marriage business, writing three best-selling books, leading our church's marriage ministry, being marriage counselors and coaches, and going around the country speaking the gospel of marriage. We also had two homes built from the ground up, purchased brand-new cars, and traveled the globe on vacation. Everything I lost and more…was restored! Nothing But God!

This book has more stories that are similar to my story that will change your life. It shows some of the things that we as men may have to overcome in our lives to be the men that God created and called us to be. I believe that when you read this book, you will not only be able to relate to some of the stories but use these stories to overcome some things in your life that you may be going through or are about to go through. My prayer is that you will realize that when all else may fail, you know whom you can turn to, and that will change everything, including the way you think or act and handle situations in life. Yes, God!

Acknowledgements

I am so thankful to God for giving me the opportunity to carry out His vision for this body of work called Yes, God meant to encourage, compel, and elevate people in the Kingdom of God to saying yes, God!

I am grateful to the seven women who helped inspire and confirm this journey with the power you brought to Yes, God Volume 1. May God continue to bless you on your journey! I thank James Greene for taking time out of your busy schedule to pour into our men and write the foreword for this book! May you and your family continue to receive endless blessings from our God!

Finally, there is no real way to fully thank the seven men enough for your time, dedication, struggle, openness, vulnerability, and courage you poured onto the pages of your chapters! I thank you for saying yes, God in your life and to this project! I thank you for your courage and your bravery! But I thank you most for allowing God to open your hearts to the desire to reach back and help another be healed and set free by sharing about your own deliverance! You all are real rock stars in the Kingdom of God!

Thanking my dad for being the first man I ever knew to stand for God!

Introduction

I'm so glad you have this book in your hands! *Yes, God! Volume 2 Men's Edition* was necessary to write because the male voice is critical in the Kingdom of God! There is a reason why the enemy did not come straight for Adam. It says a lot about the power of man in the Kingdom of God! It does not mean that the woman is not important. In fact, she is so important that God Himself said, "It is not good for man to be alone. I will make a help meet for him" (Gen 2:18 KJV). A help meet is a supporter, someone who is comparable.

The enemy has been from the beginning and still is, until this day, after the man! We were not separated from God until Adam ate the fruit. The enemy used Eve. She was deceived, the Bible tells us, to get to the man, Adam. And when Adam ate from the tree of the knowledge of good and evil, they were kicked out of the garden in the book of Genesis.

You will find the stories on these pages are of real men who have overcome real challenges, who have shown real courage, and who are committed to a real God! They speak for all men, for those of you who have ever gone through anything and feel like the enemy just won't leave you alone! They speak for all of you young men and boys out there whose father may have left you or has never been in your life. They speak for the men who have lost someone they have loved deeply and didn't think they could go on. They represent anyone who has ever been addicted to drugs or alcohol, incarcerated, confused, or just plain disobedient to God! These men were not afraid to be vulnerable, transparent, and open. May you be compelled to look inward and use the power within you to pull out what God is saying that still needs to be healed and made whole.

Each brother in this book has opened up his life so that you may truly find yours. They pray that you are encouraged to keep pressing toward the mark that God has set for you and that you never give up! They pray that if you do not know Jesus Christ for yourself, that you will come to know Him in a very personal way by accepting Him as your Lord and Savior, repenting and turning away from your sins, and confessing that Jesus is the Son of God! These men are sharing their truth so that you may know the truth, and that is that Jesus is a Savior! A Redeemer! A keeper! A healer! A deliverer! A way maker! A lover! And He will meet you right where you are!

The world is trying to silence the kingdom-minded male, especially the black kingdom-minded male. And God is saying, "My men are a critical key in the Kingdom of God. They are the head of the family! They carry the seed." Take heed to these men and all the other men out there who are not afraid to stand for Jesus Christ and tell God yes to His will! These men are far from perfect, but their yes, God attitude is helping to shape and change the world one family, one marriage, one ministry, one church, one child, and one community at a time! Join them and the fight to say yes, God!

I know when you finish reading these stories, you will be impacted, inspired, and intuitively moved to change from the inside out! I pray blessings upon blessings for you and that God will do something supernatural in your life as He has done for these few good men and so many others in the Kingdom of God who have said *yes* to God!

Love you in the most real way!
Minister Michele Noel-Peake

It Was Good That I Was Afflicted

Dominique Clark

Pain changed me for the better. The Word of God taught me how to handle pain and grow from it. That is why I'm a better man today than I was yesterday.

There are two types of pain that I want to talk about, one pain we inherit, called genetic pain, and the other pain I call grudge pain.

Genetic pain is out of our control because we were "sinful at birth" and "shapen in iniquity" (Psalm 51:5 NIV; KJV).

This means that some of us were born into broken families, generational trauma, and stuff that was passed down to us that we didn't ask for. Grudge pain is what we choose to hold on to, like being unforgiving and bitter.

To grow into the man that I am today, I had to acknowledge the fact that, yes, I was born into a mess, but God can turn it into a message. I will not use my childhood trauma as an excuse to be a messed-up person. I must be honest. The pain of my childhood trauma influenced a lot of the choices I made, such as getting locked up, doing drugs, following the wrong crowd, being in toxic relationships, and getting married and divorced at a young age.

I would also like to talk about my predisposed generational pain. Growing up, I experienced a lot of traumatic situations in my family. I am a product of divorce; I saw a lot of dysfunction in my parents' relationship while they were married. I dealt with a lot of physical abuse from my father when he disciplined my siblings and me. My mother never really intervened when my father disciplined us.

My mother and father had three children together. My twin brother, sister, and me. We were raised in the same household. My mother already had two sons before marrying my dad, and my father had two daughters and one son who passed away before marrying my mother.

The physical abuse I experienced from my father beating us really hurt me, physically and emotionally. I never felt protected by either one of my parents, and it created a lot of resentment that I still pray God heals.

I remember when my siblings and I were in elementary school. We would get sent to the nurse's office by our teacher because of the bruises and scars that were on our arms and legs from the beatings that our father would give us. The nurse would always ask us, "how did you get these bruises and scars? Is someone hurting you at home?" We would never say anything because we were so scared of what our father might do to us if we did tell her anything. She would say that if we were being hurt at home, she would call Child Protective Services. From the way she used to look at us, I could tell that she knew we weren't saying something, but since we did not say anything, she would just send us back to class.

Throughout most of my upbringing, I experienced being let down by my father. I never got rewarded when I did well. He would make so many broken promises to me. He would always tell me that if I got good grades that he would buy me a drum set. I loved playing the drums so much as a child. I never got those drums.

My father was a very gifted musician; he played the guitar. I admired my father's love for music, and that's what sometimes connected us. He wrestled with bad drug and alcohol addiction. He was always leaving the home for months at a time just to chase his drug addiction. My mom always took him back. She told us that she didn't want to raise us by herself. My father was very toxic to his children and toxic to his marriage. My older brothers on my mother's side hated my father. I remember growing up seeing my brothers try to fight my father, and that really devastated me. It really tainted my view of the family dynamic because I loved my brothers and my father, and I felt like I had to pick a side.

My father left our home permanently before I became a teenager. That really caused abandonment issues for me. Due to all of the rejection from my father, I also grew up with low self-esteem, feeling like I wasn't enough. I loved my father, and I always tried to see the best in him, but I knew from a very young age that he needed mental help.

Once my father was out of the home, that put my mom in a very tough financial situation, with three kids to support on her own. My mom worked at a DC jail as a correctional officer. She worked long hours, and we were left at home by ourselves. Since there was a lack of parental guidance and no order or structure in our home, we got into a lot of trouble.

I remember my twin brother and I decided to do an armed robbery at the age of sixteen. That was my first time going to jail. I was charged as an adult with no bond. We had to sit in jail until our trial date. My twin brother and I were separated in jail, and they put me in a twenty-three-hour lockdown unit.

That was the first time I ever talked to God. That solitary confinement really woke me up to my own pain. I cried endless tears because I knew that the cause of my actions was the root of my grudge pain. We were so angry and hurt from the abuse we experienced that we began to act out for the love that we longed for from our mother and father.

When my father was in our home, my sister, twin brother, and I were very close. After my father left for good and my mother was working long hours at the jail, we began to get into fights with each other a lot. We didn't know how to handle disagreements with each other without things getting out of hand. My siblings and I had a lot of pent-up aggression that we took out on one another.

To this day, that is something that I am still praying about because I do want a better relationship with my siblings.

My father eventually passed away when I was seventeen years old. I really didn't get the closure I wanted or the apologies that I felt I needed. I just cried about it and asked God to help me to forgive him. My twin brother, sister, and I didn't get any closer after my father died. Eventually, I got tired of getting into it with them, so I moved to my grandmother's house.

While living at my grandmother's house, I began to build a bond with my big brother on my mother's side. My big brother made me feel safe. He was a confidant. He always seemed to be a protection for me, something that I longed for from my parents.

After building such a great bond with my brother and finally having the love and protection I longed for, he was killed. This was yet another traumatizing event that occurred in my life. He died, unfortunately, at the age of twenty-four and left behind a daughter and a son.

After his death, I fell into a deep, dark depression. I didn't know which way to turn. I felt lost and confused. My family took a turn for the worst. My mom lost her job and was very depressed. This was when I began to indulge in drugs and drinking to numb my pain.

I was trying to fill that void inside of me. This was also when I began to look for love in all of the wrong places. At the age of nineteen, I got my first job and my first apartment and was shacking up with a female that I was dealing with because I did not want to deal with what was going on at my mother's house. That was not a good move at all. We had a very toxic co-dependent relationship. This relationship was built on trauma bonding, even though I didn't even know what that was at that time in my life. I dismissed every red flag because, growing up, my point of reference for relationships was my parents. So, the dysfunction that we were experiencing in our relationship was the norm for me.

I knew that I couldn't continue with that relationship, and I didn't care about breaking the lease to the apartment. As soon as I got the strength to truly walk away, she told me that she was pregnant. That is when I decided to marry her, even though deep down in my heart, I truly wanted to get out of the relationship. This was another traumatizing experience I really did not want to face, but at that point, I had no other choice.

When my son, Dominique Jr., was born, that motivated me to change. My son's birth was a pivotal point in my life. I knew that being a young dad, I needed guidance and direction on how to raise my son. I didn't know how to be a father because my father wasn't a father to me. I was willing to learn. When my son was two years old, I got saved and baptized. My first major yes to God! I joined a church, and I also joined a men's ministry group to help me grow in God. That's when I started getting the Word inside of me. God brought a whole new awareness to me.

When I started attending church regularly, I started to grow and mature in the Word. As dysfunctional as the marriage was, I decided to go to marriage counseling at the church I was a member of. Remember, I didn't want to raise my son in a broken home. The worst thing to see was him growing up with parents that do not love each other or get along and him growing up in a toxic environment as I did.

While attending marriage counseling, I discovered so many mistakes by simply moving too fast and operating in my flesh. I had to allow God to purge the self-sabotaging things out of me. The marriage counselor quoted this scripture, "Where there is no counsel, the people fall; But in the multitude of counselors there is safety" (Proverbs 11:14 NKJV).

I realized that it's important to consult God first before choosing who to marry because that sets the course of your life. I realized that I isolated myself from accountability when it came to making important decisions. I was used to doing things on my own. The Bible says, "A man who isolates himself seeks his own desire; He rages against all wise judgment. A fool has no delight in understanding, but in expressing his own heart" (Proverbs 18:1-2 NKJV). I was a fool, and once I learned to look inward instead of outward, my perspectives changed. I knew that I had to change so that I would not repeat the same cycle.

Eventually, the divorce was final, and I had split custody of my son. I focused on being a single dad. It was very tough for me. I had to go through child support, and I didn't make enough money. I didn't have a skill set, so I felt like I was at rock bottom. I had to move back into the house with my mom, which was a very humbling experience for me.

I continued to seek God and was encouraged by the brothers in my accountability group to walk in purity. That was a major struggle for me at first. I had to have a lot of hot-seat moments and accountability conversations. I started getting on prayer calls. I learned how to fast and take control of my flesh. That is when I finally started seeing the fruit of my obedience manifest.

God really started maturing me spiritually, and I developed tunnel vision with my career goals. I knew I needed to be a provider for my son, so I obtained my Commercial Driver's License (CDL), both class A and class B. Now, look at God! That was one of the most exciting times in my life to get my CDL! I always saw my family struggle for stability. I knew from that moment my life would be changed for the better. I found my confidence in Jesus Christ, which is the best place to be. Growing up with my disadvantages taught me how to be resilient.

The Bible tells us, "It was good for me to be afflicted so that I might learn your decrees" (Psalms 119:71 NIV). The affliction from my traumatic experiences is what led me to God all along. I have been let down by both of my parents, but "Though my father and mother forsake me, the Lord will receive me" (Psalms 27:10 NIV). The discipline that I received while being connected to Christ helped me tremendously. The joy that God has given me has allowed me to forgive the people who caused me pain. I also had to forgive myself.

I started making Facebook Live Bible study sermons, and I started posting scriptures on social media to encourage people. That's a passion for me to pour into people. Every time I acknowledge God in all my ways, He surely directs my path. I put God's agenda before my own, and because of that, I was able to get a good career and move out on my own. I had to learn how to totally depend on God. When I put my full focus on God, He developed me, matured me, and established me. God was showing me that He was using me to destroy the generational curses in my life.

Now I can say I know for sure that "All things work together for good to them that love God, to them who are the called according to His purpose" (Romans 8:28 KJV). Life begins to change when you understand that you are the change.

After God pushed me to grow and established me, I met a beautiful woman. She eventually became my wife. We took things slowly and courted each other for a while. What attracted me to my wife was the interest that she showed in my walk with God. She encouraged me to continue to pursue my purpose in Christ. That is where we connected. God showed me that she was going to be my wife. This time I wanted to do things the right way. Knowing I had a son, she embraced him, which was truly a blessing. My wife came with family values and a sense of togetherness, which is what I had been looking for my whole life. She was also driven career-wise and big on education. God used my wife to help me in a lot of ways when it came to showing me how to have structure with my son.

Before I proposed to her, I prayed to God and asked the Lord to please show me if this is my wife. I suggested that we should go to premarital counseling, and that is where we met Minister Peake. Premarital counseling was the best decision we made because we didn't want to go into a marriage draining each other with our past situations and baggage.

The assignments Minister Peake gave us helped us to grow together. Some conversations were very difficult to have, but the fact that we were able to communicate and talk and pray through the difficult conversations brought us even closer together than we were before we started the premarital counseling. To whom much is given, much is required. I prayed for a woman like this, so I knew that it would require a lot of me to have her. It required me to be very uncomfortable with being comfortable. Even with the things that we do not agree on, I have learned that it is okay to agree to disagree.

I am proud of us because we did the work, and God is rewarding us. We got married on May 21, 2022. We were once concerned about having a child. We prayed together and asked God to bless us with a child if it was His will. Now, I am excited to say we are expecting a baby girl! We also purchased our first home together, and we are on a trail-blazing path! I'm excited about what God has in store for us as a family.

My prayer is that God continues to align me with people who help to push me to my purpose. God specializes in using the foolish things of the world to shame the wise; God chose the weak things of the world to shame the strong. I am just an ordinary person, but God does extraordinary things with people like me. Who would have ever thought that I would successfully lead my family despite the trauma that I grew up with? I will always say yes to God's will because He knows what is best for me. I trust His purpose for my life, and I will let the Lord lead me for the rest of my life.

God Chaser

Anthony Proctor

A God Chaser is someone who has experienced the awesome electric power of the Master, Jesus Christ, who has filled them with this unimaginable and unforgettable impact on one's spirit, soul, and body. "Behold, I stand at the door and knock. If anyone hears My voice and opens the door, I will come in to him and dine with him, and he with Me" (Revelations 3:20 NKJV). I opened the door of my heart and said yes to Jesus. My journey in life is why I opened up the door of my heart.

THE BEGINNING

My older sister Vanessa and I were going to the store. I snatched my hand out of her hand and ran away from her toward the street, startling my sister. I wanted my sister to chase after me. She realized that I was running toward the street and a car was coming. She yelled my name, "Tony!" and I thought she was playing with me, so I kept running blindly toward the street, having fun. She ran after me, and just before I was about to step into the street in the path of an oncoming car, she grabbed me and pulled me back into her arms, saving my life from the oncoming car. "For He will command His angels concerning you to guard you in all your ways" (Psalms 91:11 NIV). The enemy lurks nearby for an opportunity to destroy one who is a God chaser.

The Civil Rights Act was passed in 1964, ending segregation in schools based on race, religion, national origin, sex, or color. African Americans were fighting for a rightful place in American society. Many African Americans started going to Jones Beach in Nassau County, New York, because of the Civil Rights Act.. In 1966, my mother, Mary, my brother, Terry, Vanessa, and I were on the beach having fun. Vanessa was in the water, and I was following her into the water. She went out further, and I kept on following her in the water. The ground under the water dropped down, and I went under the water. Not knowing how to swim, I was thrashing in the water, drowning, and someone grabbed me and picked me up. I was coughing and crying. Then I realized that it was Vanessa who had saved me from drowning. "When the enemy comes in like a flood, The Spirit of the Lord will lift up a standard against him" (Isaiah 59:19 NKJV). My sister was always protecting me. I reflect on those years of my life, and I realize those situations and circumstances were shaping me in my developmental years as a child. My sister made me feel safe, which helped build my courage. My mother was raising three children in New York City all by herself. Before that, she was married and had Vanessa and Terry, but her husband had abandoned her and the children. She was heartbroken, and after some time, she started a relationship with a man who was from her hometown in North Carolina. He was younger than her, but she was drawn to him, and they had me as a result of that relationship. The relationship with my father didn't work out, and my mom was brokenhearted again. I was young, but the lack of a positive male role model in my developmental years shaped my dysfunctional ways when it came to relationships with women. I never felt like I was good enough. So my mother left Washington, DC, and moved us to New York City to live close to her older sister, who lived in Hempstead, New York. She found a room in St. Albans, Queens, and then she found an apartment in St. Albans. We moved around, trying to get settled. My mother got a great job with the New York City Transit Authority, and she got another apartment in Hollis, Queens. The gangs in Hollis were overwhelming and tried to pull Vanessa into gang activity. My mother sent Vanessa back to Washington, DC, to live with my mother's younger sister.

In 1968, Martin Luther King was assassinated, and the community was in an uproar. My mother found a place in Red Hook, Brooklyn, which was 60 percent white and 11 percent black but was a safe neighborhood to live in—an African American woman with two sons in a majority-white neighborhood. The favor of God was with my mom. In spite of the state of America, she continued to take care of her family. "She watches over the ways of her household, And does not eat the bread of idleness" (Proverbs 31:27 NKJV).

My mother spent as much quality time as she could with us and, to the best of her ability, tried to teach us how to be respectful. My brother and I had to learn how to become independent without the leadership of our sister. My mother would tell us that we were the men in the family and we had to protect our home. This helped me to develop toughness, and I wanted to protect my family. In 1970, a friend of my mother's helped her find a bigger affordable place in Amityville, Long Island, and Vanessa came back home. Mom had to work long hours, and the commute was long, but Vanessa was very mature and was able to keep the house under control. I was a good student and athlete. In fifth and sixth grade, I was a kid wrestling champ and never lost a match. I went to junior high school, which is called middle school nowadays, and as a wrestler, I only lost one match.

I developed a chip on my shoulder, having anger on the inside from not having a father or a positive role model in my life. Most of my friend's fathers lived with them. My father died when I was a young teenager, and I never knew him. I went to high school and made varsity wrestling in the ninth grade because I broke the varsity wrestler's collar bone. "Stop being angry! Turn from your rage! Do not lose your temper—it only leads to harm" (Psalm 37:8 NLT). I had a lot of friends and was chasing popularity because it felt good. I was truly committed to wrestling and other sports as well. Participating in sports helped me develop a healthy respect for authority, although the racial injustice was not good in our society.

CHASING A NEW LIFESTYLE

Again we moved from Amityville in 1976 to Flushing, Queens, and I was devastated and angry. I was on a wrestling team that was so good we were forecast to go to the state championship. My coach and all of my teammates and friends were sad that I was moving away. My mother moved closer to her job because my sister and brother had both graduated from high school. The school that I went to did not have a wrestling team. My love for my mom was deep, and I wanted whatever she wanted. My life was about to change in a tremendous way. "Enter by the narrow gate; for wide is the gate and broad is the way that leads to destruction, and there are many who go in by it" (Matthew 7:13 NKJV). I made some acquaintances and started to hang out with them. One of my new acquaintances was named Jimmy, and he was a street fighter. I was a very good wrestler and fighter, so we became close friends. "Behold, how good and pleasant it is when brothers dwell in unity!" (Psalms 133:1 ESV). The grip and glamor of the streets captured us both. This was the hip-hop era, and we became DJs. There was a street hustler and pimp who sponsored us with expensive equipment, and we became known in the area by playing in parks and house parties. Drinking and drugging became part of my lifestyle. I had already been around alcohol because my sister, who was five years older than me, had to take me to the parties she went to as a teenager. I used to play music for them and was drinking alcohol at the young age of twelve. My mother was also a functional alcoholic, and alcohol was always in my home. "Wine is a mocker and beer a brawler; whoever is led astray by them is not wise" (Proverbs 20:1 NIV). I was still chasing popularity, just in a different way. I had respect on the streets, which I enjoyed. The crew I was with got into many fights with other neighborhoods and with our Caucasian brothers as well. We began to carry a small caliber pistol with us. We shared the pistol, and one of my boys had the pistol, went over to his father's house in Brooklyn, tried to rob a store, and was shot and killed by the police. Several of my boys got arrested for doing the same thing. I was an honor roll student in spite of my street reputation. I had a lady friend who was older than me, and she encouraged me to finish school. I finished high school and attended community college on grants. I felt like I was on top of the world. My mother warned me about my lady. She wanted me to take my time in that relationship, and I didn't think she knew what she was talking about. "Do not turn away from your mother's teaching" (Proverbs 1:8 NLV). My mother was right. My relationship with my lady ended, and my heart was broken. Political parties changed in our country. All of my grants went away, and

I didn't have the means to continue college. I wanted a change in my life, so I joined the military.

This is similar to what my mother did in her failed relationships—she ran away and never really dealt with them. When we don't face our brokenness, it causes us to build up resentment. This, along with other life circumstances, is probably one of the reasons my mother was a functional alcoholic. She medicated her brokenness with alcohol and dead-end relationships.

I was not walking with the Lord. I watched my mother pray every night, and she taught me, my brother, and my sister how to pray. My mother prayed for all of her children, and I had no idea that God's hand was keeping me. I joined the Air Force, and along with my school education and having street savvy, I was confident for all of the wrong reasons. I was committed to everything I was involved in. Because of my college success, I was placed in a leadership role in the Air Force. I continued to chase popularity, and as a DJ, I played in clubs. I also began to sell illegal substances, and became very popular. I got married and thought I was successful.

"For as he thinks in his heart, so is he. 'Eat and drink!' he says to you, But his heart is not with you." (Proverbs 23:7 NKJV). My drinking was very progressive, and it destroyed my marriage. I got into a lot of trouble, getting arrested and enduring the disease of alcoholism. I came out of the Air Force and moved to Washington, DC, where my mother was now living. "On that day I raised My hand in an oath to them, to bring them out of the land of Egypt into a land that I had searched out for them, 'flowing with milk and honey,' the glory of all lands" (Ezekiel 20:6 NKJV).

CHASING THE NEW BEGINNING

My mother was living in the ghetto. I moved my mother and the rest of my family out of that neighborhood into a better one. I immediately got a job as a letter carrier in the US Postal Service. "If anyone will not work, neither shall he eat" (2 Thessalonians 3:10 NKJV). My mother was a great example of a hard worker. I got a job earning decent money. I became popular in the postal service. Continuing as a DJ and working for the local union helped me develop my desire to help people in need. My drinking and drug use was progressive and caused me to have many problems. I remember an experience while drinking. I got in my car to drive home. I was on the road, and I saw lights coming toward me on the same side of the road I was on. I realized that I was on the wrong side of the road of an interstate parkway. I turned the wheel and was able to go over to the other side of the parkway. "As he journeyed he came near Damascus, and suddenly a light shone around him from heaven" (Acts 9:3 NKJV). This experience opened my eyes to seek help for my drinking and drug use—little did I know that God's Hand was orchestrating the direction I was going.

I spoke to a neighbor who took me to his church, where they had a 12-step program. The program helped me see that I needed God in my life. I accepted Jesus Christ as a result of attending those 12-step meetings and going to that church. Everything in my life turned around. I got custody of my daughter and met a woman named Jean, who had two children. We began to see one another, and she came to the church that I was going to and became a member. We went to Bible study together and were building a strong relationship with God. One night coming out of Bible study, she got into the car with her son. I went to pick up a young guy I was mentoring. On my way to get the young guy, a large pickup truck ran the light and broadsided my car. I don't remember the accident, and I was hospitalized for over a week in critical condition. God protected me from that accident and healed me. After that experience, Jean, who could have been in my car that night, became my wife, and we are now servants of the Lord Jesus Christ locally and internationally. "For the word of God *is* living and powerful, and sharper than any two-edged sword, piercing even to the division of soul and spirit, and of joints and marrow, and is a discerner of the thoughts and intents of the heart" (Hebrews 4:12 NKJV). The Word of God helped us come together as man and wife.

The Word of God helped me to fall in love with and begin to chase after Jesus Christ. I became a teacher of the Word of God, and I chased the study and understanding of the Word of God. Chasing as a servant, God ordained me as a Deacon, and after a while, I was licensed as a Minister. I preached His Word locally and internationally. My wife became licensed as a Minister. I looked over my life, and I realized that God's Hand had been keeping me and directing me to become an instrument of His. The kind of life that I was living from my foundational years through my school years was shaping me to become the type of man that I have become. I now minister to alcoholics, drug users, returning citizens, and homeless people.

I look back on an experience my sister went through in college, being beaten up by her boyfriend. God protected me from myself as I was unable to find the guy who beat her up. This has helped me to have a heart for the victims of domestic violence. "We are hard-pressed on every side, yet not crushed; we are perplexed, but not in despair; persecuted, but not forsaken; struck down, but not destroyed" (2 Corinthians 4:8-9 NKJV). Being a part of those who help domestic violence victims is a ministry that is deep in my heart. Chasing after God has developed and grown me over the years by having a committed prayer life. I no longer hate my father because God has shown me how to forgive him and my mother. I found out that I have a younger sister from my father's side of the family. The generational curses of resentment, brokenness, unforgiveness, parental abandonment, alcoholism, and substance use disorder have been broken by this relationship with Jesus Christ. "Confess your trespasses to one another, and pray for one another, that you may be healed. The effective, fervent prayer of a righteous man avails much" (James 5:16 NKJV).

I am now an ordained pastor, walking in the calling that God has called me to. Overcoming and still going through many challenges in my life has helped me to continue to trust and believe in Jesus Christ and His saving grace and mercies in my life. He has given me the courage to "walk by faith, not by sight" (2 Corinthians 5:7 NKJV), recognizing that Jesus is committed to me and His church. "For the Word of the Lord is right and true; He is faithful in all He does" (Psalm 33:4 NIV). Walking in the will and the way of God has helped me to live in His truth, and this is the reason why my lifestyle of *Being a God Chaser* has allowed me to say yes to God!

He Saved Me Before He Saved Me

Harold Ferrell

"Man who *is* born of woman is of few days and full of trouble."—Job 14:1 (NKJV)

When I look back over my life, I have had lots of trouble. Trouble followed me from my teen years right into adulthood, most of which was by my own doing. It was the *trouble* in my life that would eventually lead me to an important "Yes," along this journey. My siblings and I were raised by a single mother. She made sure we had food to eat and a place to live. She worked hard, taught us right from wrong, and did not get much if any, help from my father. He and my mother divorced not long after I was born, and I know it was not easy for her as she struggled to raise five kids.

I was the oldest and had many responsibilities helping to take care of my sister and brothers. As I grew older, I began to rebel, causing much friction and grief for my mother. I had a bad attitude, and I was selfish. I lied, cheated, and stole in an attempt to get what I wanted. Whenever I was caught or called out on my behavior, I always had someone else to blame. You see, I didn't want to take any responsibility for my actions, and I had an excuse for everything. Life was hard, and fairness didn't exist—at least for me. It would be so easy for me to say I didn't know any better, but that would have been a lie—a futile and misguided attempt to even out the playing field just for me.

I said my mother didn't get much help from my dad. The truth is she didn't get any help from him. My first memory of him is one day when he just showed up and took me to meet his side of the family. I met his sister, her husband and daughter, and then another sister and her daughter. I believe I was about nine years old. I didn't really get much from my dad in the way of a father-son relationship. He didn't teach me any of the things a father should teach his son.

For one thing, he was a military man and served most of his time in faraway places. Another thing was that he didn't try to establish a relationship with me. After he completed his army career, I did get the opportunity to see him a little more often, but it didn't bring us any closer together. Aside from the fact that he was my father, in retrospect, I never got the one thing I needed most in my life, and that was the father-son bond. He was not the strong black male role model I needed in my life. I can see how it may sound like I'm judging. I am not passing judgment. I'm just stating a cold, hard fact.

I began to get into trouble with the law when I was a teenager. Somewhere around the age of thirteen, I was skipping school one day with a friend, and we decided to look at some cars parked at a gas station. One of the cars had a broken-out window, which we did not break. We were standing there looking inside the car when a man showed up asking, "What are you doing?" And we took off running! My friend got away, and I got caught. This was my first encounter with the law, but it wasn't my last. I had several more incidents that were mostly petty in nature. I know this caused my mother lots of grief.

My mother was a single mother at a very young age. She was seventeen and married when I was born. By the time she was twenty-three, she had three children and very little support from her family. We were poor, but she made the rent every month, so we were never out of a place to live. Yes, we were a poor family, but we were a family. I don't ever remember having an empty table or being hungry. Mommy worked hard, and she loved her children. She worked hard to earn her certification as a Licensed Practical Nurse (LPN). She worked the majority of her career on the overnight shift at the university hospital. Sunday mornings, she would come home and get us dressed for Sunday school and church. After breakfast, she would send us off to the church down the street, and she would try to get some sleep. Usually, we would spend the few coins she gave us for church donations on bubblegum and penny candy.

As we grew older, we didn't go to church often. I believed God was real, but I had no true knowledge of Him or His Son, Jesus. Long before my salvation, I would even pray for his help at times, like the time I was in jail for participating in the burglary of a neighborhood meat market. I was also definitely thanking Him after being robbed at gunpoint as I worked the register at my neighborhood convenience store. As I looked down the barrel of that 38-revolver pointed at me, I know I stopped breathing, and I could literally hear my heart pounding inside my chest. He has been my protector from the beginning.

My ultimate "Yes God" has been a journey that began at a young age. Growing from adolescence into adulthood handed me some life experiences that would ultimately shape me, mold me, and show me how much I needed God in my life. I was a lost soul with many character flaws that kept me from being the man God created me to be. I was chosen by Him to be His son, His child, in His kingdom.

As a man, I would have many responsibilities. A man is to lead—period. I was chosen by God to be the firstborn of five, and as such, I was the big brother. Big brothers have a responsibility to lead and protect their siblings. God also chose me to be a husband. Initially, I failed at this too. I was born to be the father of three beautiful children. I struggled to be a good big brother, good husband, and good father. It all suffered due to selfishness, pridefulness, laziness, impulsiveness, and a thick head—my life was all about me.

It's hard to be a good husband, father, son, and brother when your priorities in life are all wrong. You see, I lived a good part of my young life smoking cigarettes, using pot, and drinking beer almost every day. I first smoked marijuana when I was a senior in high school. Later, I also picked up cigarettes as a habit. From that point on, through four years of college and into my late twenties, I was a regular smoker. When you smoke every day, you spend a lot of time trying to run down your next good batch. It becomes an ongoing chore that consumes a lot of time and energy. It was all-consuming. I would do just about anything to score some more weed. Marijuana was my drug of choice, but I would experiment with other substances. I tried cocaine, acid, and even crack cocaine. It was by the love and grace of God that I wasn't hooked on the hard stuff. You see, my allergies—the allergies that caused me so much grief—weren't conducive to snorting cocaine. I suffered all my life with extreme allergies, so taking drugs through my nostrils just led to other less desirable outcomes. I once snorted some cocaine, and my nose was literally like a running faucet that couldn't be shut off for nearly three days! Most of that time was spent stuffing tissue in my nostrils every two minutes. These side effects were too severe to continue and outweighed any high I could get. It was not meant for me to be a "cokehead." I believe marijuana was the natural choice for me because I didn't like the hangover from drinking liquor. I drank beer because it was somewhat easier to handle than hard liquor. My experiments with other substances were short-lived, as I had adverse reactions to all of them. I tried PCP, which made me extremely nauseous and so high that I had no control over my mind or body. I tried crack cocaine multiple times but never experienced that euphoric high that enslaved so many others. It may have been that I didn't come in contact with the real thing, or maybe it was God who wouldn't allow me to become an addict. So many people get hooked with the first try. Why not me? When I was saying yes to drugs and alcohol, God was saying no. Thank you, Jesus!

Using and experimenting with drugs took its toll. I had the opportunity to be the first one in my family to graduate from college. When I left for college, it was my first time being away from home, and I couldn't handle it. I didn't know anyone, I wasn't prepared, and I didn't have a local support system. I met some new friends, and the party was on. That was my focus, partying, chasing girls, and smoking marijuana. School took a back seat to everything. I didn't have any discipline or structure, and with no clearly defined objectives and goals, college appeared to be a wasted opportunity. After four years of college, I was no closer to graduating than the day I stepped on campus.

At some point, I could see that I needed to make some changes in my life. A change of scenery was needed. I moved to Atlanta, where my high school sweetheart was living after she left college. We began to live together with plans to get married and have children. There was one major problem, though. I had no idea or clue what that meant. It didn't take long for us to figure out that we didn't really know each other very well. Our relationship was severely strained, and I didn't know what to do about it. I lost multiple jobs, and when I was working, I had trouble managing money. It seemed as if we were always under the threat of eviction. In fact, the day came when we were days from being evicted from our apartment. This led to a brief separation in which she went to stay with a family member, and I returned home to my mother. After our short time apart, we did get back together and attempted to make our relationship work again. In the transition from my mother's house to getting back with my future wife, I rented a room at a rooming house where I lived for a couple of weeks.

A few months after reuniting, we found out we were having a baby. My son was born, and I was now a father. I was young and needed to grow up fast, but I was having trouble living up to my responsibility. I felt having a son would draw us closer together, but it didn't. I always dreamed of being married and being a father to my son, unlike my father, but our relationship was crumbling fast, and my dream was not going to happen. I was always going to be a father to my son but I was not living in the manner God intended.

I didn't want our relationship to end, but she was ready for it to be over. I was under a lot of stress at the time. It seemed like I was always between jobs, and money was tight. I was struggling to make sense of my situation, and I was at a very low point in my life. Even then,

I was praying for God to help me, to rescue me from my despair. Little did I know I was well on my way to my "Yes, God."

During the two weeks I spent at that rooming house, I made a lifelong friend named Ed. He had recently finished his service in the army and had come to Atlanta to settle down. We became good friends. God brought Ed into my life at that rooming house so that I would say "yes," to accept Jesus as my Lord and Savior. It was good for me to meet Ed at that time. I didn't really have anyone in whom I could confide. I wasn't the type to confide in anyone about problems in my life, and I was probably too easygoing for my own good. I tended to ignore problems or just bury my head in the sand until it was all clear. I would always try to take the easy way. I was young, lazy, and did not like hard work—definitely not a very good way to manage my life.

My life was a mess, and I could not ignore that fact. I was a father now, and as I said earlier, I needed to grow up. I said to myself that I was going to be a better dad for him than my father was to me. I had to have something to teach my son other than taking the easy way. There is no such thing as easy. A good work ethic is paramount. My mother was an excellent living example of that. She made sacrifices for us, and she worked hard every day to care for and feed her children. I knew I needed to make some sacrifices and work as hard as I could, but when and how was this going to happen? I was clearly at a crossroads in my life, and I would need to make some life changes.

Over the course of several months, Ed would minister to me. He had grown up as the son of a preacher and would later become a minister. He encouraged me to start going to church and to read the Bible. He wanted me to start saying no to some of the things in my life that kept me down. Getting high every day didn't do anything to get me where I needed to be. His position was that things would get better if I accepted Christ into my life. He would constantly invite me to Sunday service and mid-week Bible study. He would say to me, "all you have to do is accept Jesus into your life and the Holy Spirit will do the rest. I know you're ready for a change in your life." I was ready for a change in my life, but I couldn't seem to get out of my own way. I was stuck on saying no to God. Friends and family would invite me to church and Bible study, and I would kindly decline. Most of the time, I would tune them out and be ready to say no at the right time. I needed to find some courage from somewhere and say yes, God. I believe he did save me from some of my bad behaviors and habits even before I received salvation. I could have easily been an addict, but He didn't allow it.

Ed was an encouragement to me and prayed for me. But he knew it had to be my choice. Saying yes is personal and has to be of your own free will. God was offering me a way out of my situation, and I needed to be able to recognize it and accept it. I had to decide what kind of man I wanted to be. On my own, I had made a mess of my life.

One Sunday morning, there was a knock at the door, and it was Ed. He walked in and said, "get dressed and come go to church with me. I ain't taking no for an answer. You need to do this." Somewhat reluctantly, I got dressed and went to church with him. I didn't really know what to expect. In terms of the actual service and the word that the preacher gave, I don't remember any of it. But what I will never forget is what happened toward the end. I must have been sitting there with all of my troubles plus those of half the world on my face, because the preacher looked at me and said, "young man, I can look at you and see it all over your face. You need Jesus! Get up, young man, and see the grace of God." I got up out of my seat and went up to the front and stood before the preacher. She asked me my name and a few other questions. Then she asked if I was ready to be saved. My yes came at that moment. She led me in the prayer of salvation. "Dear Father God, I am a sinner, and please forgive me. I believe Jesus is Your Son and died for my sins and you raised Him from the dead. Please come into my life. I trust You as my Lord and Savior." I was twenty-seven years old. My time had come to say yes, God!

On the way home, Ed said he was happy for me. He told me that from now on, God would fight my battles. My job now was to trust Him and learn as much as I could about the Lord, read my Bible and learn how to pray, and let the Holy Spirit lead. From time to time, I reflect on that day and am in wonder at what God did when he showed that preacher there was a soul ready to say yes.

As time went on, I came to learn about God and develop a relationship with Him. I still had some issues that needed attention. God's grace caused me to quit smoking marijuana. I probably did drink hard liquor more than before, but it wasn't abusive. The one habit that caused me the most concern was cigarette smoking. I began in my early twenties, and as I grew older, I began to realize it was time to give that up, also. It took me waking up one Friday morning short of breath. As I got out of the bed to start my day, breathing became more laborious. I felt like my time might be up. I slowly got dressed and went to my doctor's office, only to find he didn't come into the office on Fridays. I left there disappointed and returned to another doctor who had cared for me in the past. It turned out to be a bad case of bronchitis. But that day was the catalyst for me to give up tobacco. I had tried many times in the past to quit. I think I was able to go anywhere from a week to maybe two months without smoking. All it took for me to give in and pick it up again was some kind of stress. But this time was different. As I lay on my bed one day, I began to pray to God to take away the desire to smoke. I asked Him to strengthen me with His strength. He did. I was able to quit. Early on, whenever the urge to smoke came, I would say a prayer, and the urge would leave me. Hallelujah!

It was the grace of God that brought stability, growth, maturity, and love to my life. He gave me a loving wife and children. He did it, not me. When I tried to be in control of my life, I failed. Once I turned my life over to him, things changed, and I was changed.

Fast forward to my present years. I am a brand-new man. I am not a perfect man, but a God-fearing man. I don't walk alone. God walks with me. He guides me and directs my path. He had been there all along. If he didn't hear my unsaved, teenage, and young adult prayers, I know He definitely heard the prayers of those saints who prayed for me because He saved me. Through it all, God didn't change—I did. I don't just have *knowledge* of Him—I know Him. I have a relationship with Him. I spend time with Him every day. Shouldn't you spend time with those you love? He has always been faithful, and now I place my faith in Him. I am no longer the young man who drank alcohol and internalized drugs. I am now the man who drinks the blood of Jesus, and He lives in my heart.

I played tug of war with you, God, for years: I first said *no* to your yes, then said *maybe* to your yes, and then freely gave my "Yes, God" to constant Yes!

That's when You saved me!... *And then* You *saved* me. Hallelujah!

How God Used Me and Kept Me Through the Loss and Grief of My Wife

Grayling V.G. Sterling Sr.

OUR LOVE

I fell in love with her when I first laid eyes on her. We were nine years old. She had fire-red hair, which she wore in pigtails, and had on cat eyeglasses. She had the biggest and brightest smile that I had ever seen and a heart to match. We would hang out together all the time, and we became the best of friends. I knew back then that she would one day be my wife. She lived two houses down from me. As a teenager, I found myself at her house quite often. It became my second home. After I graduated from high school, I joined the service. I thought of her often when I would come home on leave. I somehow never managed to see her, though. And when I would go over to her parent's house, I would ask about her, and they would tell me that she was doing well.

Fast-forward about twenty years. One day, I came home and went to visit her family. To my surprise, her mother told me that she had just gotten off the phone with her and that she was on her way over. So, I said I would wait. It had been a long time since I had seen her. The doorbell rang, her mother opened the door, and I heard her voice. She had no idea that I was there. When I saw her, I was overjoyed. It was like I had stepped back in time! It was like looking at an angel! She was amazing! We embraced each other with the biggest hug, and her smile lit up the room.

We talked and got to know each other all over again, catching up on our lives. A couple of years later, as fate would have it, I got divorced, and she became a widow. We reconnected again after a couple of years. We got married and were living our lives like most couples. We bought a home; we were active in our church and living our best life. We did everything together. We were very happy. You wouldn't see one without the other. I couldn't imagine my life without her. She was my world.

STORM'S BREWING

One day, about a week after my sixtieth birthday, my wife's eyes were yellow. We went to the doctor, and he sent us to get lab work and some other tests. Based on the tests, they made an appointment for a Cat Scan. That's when they saw she had a mass on her pancreas. They took a sample to test it, and it came back positive. They told me the woman I had loved all my life was diagnosed with pancreatic cancer.

To make matters worse, we were told that it was inoperative. It was like someone stabbed me in my heart and twisted the knife. It was then that my world, as I knew it started to fall apart. Still in shock, I couldn't believe what

I had just heard and was not sure how I would be able to handle it. But I knew I had to be strong for her, and I didn't want my wife to suffer in any form or fashion. My wife was a very health-conscious person. She was fit and exercised all the time. She ate properly and was a vegan. We really could not understand how or where this diagnosis came from. We started searching for solutions for healing holistically.

TRUSTING GOD

So, I turned to God and prayed for her strength and courage, along with not having to suffer. Being the man that I am, I wanted to protect her and take on anything that would cause her harm. At this point, I felt useless because I was unable to protect the woman I loved. I felt like my hands were tied. I also asked God to let me take her place to relieve her of her burden. He told me that it wasn't for me. I was devastated and heartbroken. At that point, I realized it was out of my hands. I had to trust God totally. Because she was very health conscious, we weren't just going to accept what they said. We were in search of and looking for the best ways for her to get treatment besides chemo. We searched for other doctors and found an herbalist. My wife was very strong and would carry herself as if nothing was wrong. I admired that about her. She made it look easy even though it was not. She was not one to complain.

GOING THROUGH A STORM

As time went by, I watched her literally wither away to skin and bones. It was tearing me up inside to see my beautiful wife deteriorate to almost nothing. But I knew that I still had to be strong for her despite how I felt inside. Even with the consecutive losses of family members, she remained strong and smiled. She lost her grandmother, great-aunt, and her mother, which I believe exacerbated her illness even more. I let her know that she had my support 1,000 percent.

We went on our last trip together and drove down to Myrtle Beach, South Carolina. She wanted to see and be near the ocean. She was very weak, so we spent our time together in the room watching the ocean, along with the sunrise and sunset. It was a beautiful time together.

GIVING BACK TO GOD

Once we got back home from Myrtle Beach, I had to take my wife to the hospital because she became very sick, and the prognosis was not good. I was told to call our family, so I did, and I also called the church. Everyone came to the hospital. The church came with a bus full of people. It was standing room only in her room, and everyone couldn't fit inside. But we had church in the hospital!

I stayed the night with my wife in her room, not knowing if she was going to pull through. She woke up in the middle of the night and called to me. I answered. I told her I loved her and that I had no regrets about our life together. She wanted to walk, so we walked down the hall and sat down by a window for a bit, where she peacefully rested in my arms. The next morning, she woke up feeling like herself, as if nothing was wrong. Even the doctors were amazed. It goes to show you that man is not in charge.

After seeing her, the doctors said there was nothing else they could do except make her as comfortable as possible. They were going to be releasing her from the hospital under hospice. I became her caregiver. We would talk about our time together and reminisce about the old days.

Most importantly, we were professing our love for one another. I would assist her to the chair, bed, etc. Whenever she wanted to move, I would tell her OK. We would dance to wherever it was that she wanted, and she liked that. I was there for her at every call.

I decided to have a talk with God about my wife and me. I said to God that I would gladly take her place. Again, He told me it wasn't for me. So, I said to God, "OK. I know that she's not mine and that you only loaned her to me as a steward to care for her on this earth. I know she's your daughter, and you can take care of her much better than I ever could. I am grateful for the time you have blessed us with each other in our lives together.

Even though I don't want to let her go, I give her back to you because I trust you, and I know that you are able."

GOD'S CALLING

After fighting for nine months, my wife of sixteen years succumbed to her illness.

On that day, we had our last dance together, and she collapsed in my arms. That was when my world ended. I had nothing else to live for at that point in my life. I really didn't care about myself or anything. I had lost my best friend. My soulmate. I had nothing in my life to live for. Our world had come to an end. All of our family were there. They tried to get me to leave the house, saying I shouldn't be there alone. I told them that I was fine and that I was staying in my home.

Once everyone left, I was thinking back over my life with my wife and how much it hurt, and how much I missed her. I cried myself to sleep most nights. But during my time of grieving, I turned more to God. On the day that my wife transitioned, all the strength, courage, and things that I had prayed for her…God gave all of that to me and more. He gave me that peace that only He can provide.

I could have turned in any direction, meaning being angry, drinking, and causing harm to myself by not caring about anything or anybody, but God kept me. I found His Word to be true. He said he would never leave me or forsake me. I entrenched myself in His word where he kept me. He showed me and helped me during my time of mourning and my loss and grief. He gave me my peace beyond all understanding because I was reading His Word and seeking direction and answers to what God had for me. His Word became inspirational and my therapy for helping me heal.

LIVING WITHOUT MY LIFE PARTNER

After laying my wife to rest and everything was over and done, I had come to terms with the fact that my life as I knew it had changed, even though that was not what I wanted. It was a reality check. I was facing a new normal. A life without my wife. I still was not ready to let her go. Looking back, I recognize that I was somewhat in denial. I could still hear her voice and laughter and see her smile, all of which made me miss her even more. It was like having an open wound that wouldn't heal right away. It was a very lonely time for me. I was alone in my house, barely living. I was thinking and remembering our lives together and crying myself to sleep, knowing that she was no longer here with me. I now realize that God was carrying me during that time.

I decided to go to Seattle to spend some time with my sons. The trip did help me to take my mind off my situation a little, but when I came back home, the loneliness set in again. My house didn't feel the same. It didn't have that warmth that it used to have. I did not like that. It's hard to get through a loss when you see people who remind you of that loss everywhere you go. Everyone means well, but sometimes you must process the situation by yourself. Just you and God. So again, I had to humble myself and go to God with my troubles. He helped me by showing me how to deal with grief and loneliness through His Word. I had a Bible app I was using, which I found to be very helpful. It had Bible plans in it that helped me to understand and grasp the rollercoaster of emotions I was going through. I found several plans to read that helped me deal with loneliness, grief, and loss. I would even recommend those plans and the Bible app to anyone who is finding themselves going through any situation in life. I see now that I was putting God first. By me putting God first, I surrendered to Him completely. That is what really opened the way for God to come and work with and on me.

DOING GOD'S WILL

During my time using the Bible app for my healing process, God assigned me to spread His Word. I thought, what better way to spread His Word than through social media? I was obedient as He led me to create words of inspiration to encourage others, as it had done for me.

The encouragement I send out is called *God's Word.* I strongly believe that this is my calling from God to do His will and to spread His Word everywhere. And I send it out daily without fail to Twitter, Facebook, and Instagram platforms, as well as through individual text messages to different people.

SAYING YES TO GOD

After about two years, I felt like I wanted a companion. Someone I could hang out with, talk to, and more. I wanted to be fair to the person I was going to be with, wondering how I could love someone else when I was still completely in love with my late wife. So I went to my mother and asked her that very same question. She told me all I could do was to just love that person for who they are. It made a lot of sense to me. I started dating. It was totally different from when I was much younger. Because I don't drink or go to clubs, I decided to try online dating. I signed up on a couple of sites. It was a whole new world.

I found myself seeing different women, and they were not all good experiences. It was getting costly. I say that because I am a gentleman and a firm believer in treating a woman like a lady. Opening doors, pulling out chairs, paying for dates, etc. I grew tired of that quickly. I had reached a point where I needed to stop doing the dating thing. I didn't like what I was becoming, seeing different women every week or on the weekends. I was looking for someone I could connect with and be myself. I wasn't trying to be a player or anything like that. I was not into playing high school games. I just wanted someone that was down to earth, not fake, or desperate just to have a man, or to see what a man can do for her, or to see what I have.

I said a prayer to God, "Lord, you know me, you made me, you know what I like and what I don't like. I'm giving it to you, who do you want me to be with." Before I could finish saying Amen, the good Lord showed me the lady that He wanted me to have in my life. When I saw her picture, I said, "Lord, you got jokes!" She was too beautiful to be on a dating site. After two weeks of wrestling with the Lord and making excuses for why I could not reach out to her, I humbled myself to do His will. I am so glad that I said yes to Him. If I had not, I would have missed my blessing. God always knows best!

RESTORATION

I believe that since I've been faithful and obedient to God, even when I thought I didn't have a purpose anymore, God has shown me that I do have a purpose. He has shown me that my purpose is to serve Him. He has shown me His favor. He has blessed me beyond anything that I could have imagined. I thought that I would never marry again. But God had other plans, and truth be told, His plan is the only plan that matters. He has blessed me with a new wife. Yes, the same one that I was wrestling with Him over. She is a God-fearing woman who loves the Lord. A woman who loves me for who I am and not for what I have. She's everything that I asked for and more. I'm so glad that I was obedient to God. The woman God chose for me is phenomenal. She's understanding, compassionate, caring, sympathetic, and drop-dead Gorgeous. Most of all, she's a woman of God and my angel.

I didn't think that I would ever feel for anyone the way I felt for my late wife, and yet, here she was in the flesh! She had stolen my heart. There is nothing that I would not do for this woman. He didn't stop there, though. His blessings continued by blessing us with a new home before we got married and upgrading us to a better home just two years after we got married. That's what I call pouring out blessings that you don't have room enough to receive. And if anyone had told me that this was going to happen, I wouldn't have believed them. I know without a doubt that there is a God, and His Word is truth!

GLORIFYING GOD

What would my life be like without God being first and foremost in it? God only knows where I would be. I have come to know and trust God for myself. I know His promise is true, and He is a way-maker. After going through everything I have gone through over these last several years, I now know how Job felt! I'm a living witness that God is still in the healing and blessing business.

I love God so much that I can't even explain it. His grace and mercy endure forever. I'm thankful to him for this opportunity and the privilege of being on this project. My prayer is that my experience will be able to benefit someone else who may be in a struggle with a loss or somehow see that they too can get through life even when it looks hopeless. The key is to have faith in all that you do. Trust in God always, no matter what you are going through. He will not steer you wrong.

Today, I can easily say that I am definitely a man of faith! Without my faith and trust in God, I would be nothing but a lost soul. I am so grateful that I am one of his own. And even more grateful that God kept me and is using me. Hallelujah! I give Him all praise and honor!!

The love of God is so powerful that it can lead you, keep you, and use you when you think you have nothing left. I am still amazed at His keeping power no matter what I face in life.

Yes, And...

Andre Reynolds

Yes, and...This is the foundation of all improvisational comedy. It makes it possible for anything to happen. For example, if your improv partner suggests that the two of you are cowboys and your shoelaces are ropes, the appropriate answer is, "Yes, and...let's lasso some cattle while riding our imaginary flying horses." You see? That's the beauty and magic of yes, and...

We will get back to Yes, and...a little later, and you'll see how and why it's played a major role in my life and, more importantly, me saying yes to God.

It was July 2010. I was sitting in my car in Branch Brook Park in Newark, NJ, the same park in which I had played as a child. Fond memories of laughter and smiles faded as I realized that I was just a sad man holding on to memories of better days. I sat there wondering how I ended up in this situation, all alone, with very little money. I had been sleeping in my youngest brother's basement after being betrayed by the two people I had loved and trusted the most. This was one of the lowest points in my life, and I was trying to figure out how and why this had happened to me. In the words of the great philosopher Jay-Z, "It was all good just a week ago."

It really did seem like just a week ago that I was on top of the world. I had a beautiful family, wonderful kids, a healthy bank account, and friends and family who adored and respected me. I enjoyed success in the corporate world and was a business owner. Then all of a sudden, I found myself downsized, out of a job, and no longer a business owner. This all happened simultaneously as the betrayals occurred. A perfect storm of *what the heck?* I won't share the sordid details of the betrayals. The reason for that is twofold. First, I have found a way to forgive those individuals, and second, I came to realize that I had no control over what they did. I cannot blame them for their choices, but I do take responsibility for what I allowed them to do to me and how I responded. Just know that some real funky stuff went down, and before I knew it, I was sobbing in my car.

After a while, I started thinking about a very close friend of mine who had committed suicide a few years prior. From my perspective, her life appeared to be great. So, I never understood why anyone, especially her, could do such a thing. However, I had reached a level of depression that made me understand. I didn't want to hurt myself, but I understood. I just didn't want to be here anymore. I stopped wanting to be here long before I ended up in the park. I'm not sure if that was the real reason I went there. I was confused but what I was sure of was that a lot of people would be profoundly affected and hurt if I were no longer around. If not for that thought and my recently growing relationship with God at the time, I quite possibly would not be here today.

A strange thing happened that day. As I just said, my relationship with God had been growing stronger just before everything went crazy in my life. He was still the one constant good in my life. I was just starting to realize that all of the good fortune I was enjoying before things went dark was because of God's grace and mercy. I always had a sense that good things were happening to me. Even when bad times came, I knew that somehow things would work out. Somehow in my brilliance, I didn't make the connection that it was God all the time. This time, however, was different. I saw no way out. And as the one in my circle that everyone came to for help, advice, money, etc., I felt like I had no one to turn to. In hindsight, it actually was not true at all. I knew I had family and friends I could turn to. I was just too embarrassed to ask for help or even to share what was really going on. My ego would not allow it. Hence, the growing depression. That same ego kept me from even turning to God. So, God revealed Himself to me in a way I had never experienced up until that point. He asked, "Do you Love me?" He also asked, "Do you trust me?" This was my first opportunity to say yes to God!

1 John 4:19 NIV states, "We love because He first loved us." I believe this to be true. Although not in scripture, I also believe that we should say yes to God because He says yes to us all the time. In retrospect, even his "no"

somehow becomes a "yes." Kind of like Romans 8:28 KJV, which reads, "And we know that all things work together for good to them that love God, to them who are the called according to his purpose."

God's timing is perfect, so we should just accept it. It may feel slow at times, but that's our human impatience, so trust that if you got your yes any faster than God granted it, you probably would not be happy with the outcome. However, sometimes that perfect timing is so fast that it can make your head spin.

Around the time when things were going haywire for me, I had the prospect of a new job that I believed was going to fix everything. My thinking was, "of course, I always find a way. Things always work out." How foolish I was to think that even if *my* plan did manage to work out and fix everything, that it was I who would deserve the credit, aka praise.

Those of a particular age may remember the financial crisis of 2009/2010, America's worst financial state since the Great Depression. Well, along with leading to my downsizing from a company that I served for seventeen years, the crisis also foiled my super plan for redemption. After I was laid off, I still had a thriving business that didn't require a lot of hands-on work from me, so I decided to start substitute teaching to deal with the boredom of being a stay-at-home dad while my daughters were in school. It also allowed me to spy on them since I only subbed at their school. It certainly wasn't my plan, but

I developed a love for teaching and decided to go back to school to become a real teacher. After completing my teaching program, I was promised a lead teacher position at the preschool where I was working as an assistant teacher. That was the plan. Starting in September, I would be a real teacher with a real teacher's salary. I thought I was back in the game, right? Wrong. Due to the financial crisis, my director lost the funding for the classroom that was going to be mine. If I stayed there, she could only continue to pay me the assistant teacher wages. "This can't be," I thought to myself. This had been my plan to fix everything. Shortly after this addendum to the perfect storm, I found myself at the park. Thankfully, after saying yes to God, the real plan was revealed.

I started applying for teaching jobs in the surrounding school districts. I was determined to make my plan work. I couldn't get an interview anywhere. Then a friend told me that a company was recruiting American teachers to work overseas in a place called the United Arab Emirates (UAE). The what? All I knew was that it was in the Middle East, and they were paying a lot of money. The money part fit my plan. The Middle East, though, not so much. OK, God, you're playing with me, right? Despite my reasoning that I would never get such a job because I was freshly certified to teach, and surely this opportunity was for more experienced teachers, to shut my friend up and to prove that God would not want me to travel to such a great unknown, I applied for a position in Abu Dhabi. Within a week, I had a Skype interview. Who remembers Skype? Within two weeks, I was in New York for an in-person interview, and before I knew it, I had a job offer and a first-class flight to Abu Dhabi. All I had to do was accept the offer. It was an incredible offer. Almost double the salary I was expecting to earn as a first-year teacher in NJ, housing paid for by the company, and flights back and forth during the summers and holiday breaks. This was better than my plan, except for the whole Middle East thing.

Now, I had to tell my family. I didn't feel the need to tell anyone sooner because up until I had an offer, it wasn't real. Clearly, everyone thought I had lost my mind for even considering this. I struggle to remember anyone who supported the idea of going to a foreign country none of us had even heard of before. I turned to God and said, are you sure? What about my children? What about the marriage I was still trying to salvage? What if I fail? How can I possibly succeed over there? Then once again, I heard those words, "Do you Trust me?" Yes, God, but I'm scared. After dealing with the backlash of family and friends, who I am sure had only the best of intentions when expressing their apprehensions, I decided that this leap of faith required extra prayer. I had only days left to accept the offer before it was rescinded. I went to church that Sunday, and as if I had any business bargaining with God, I said, if you really want me to go, give me your final answer during the sermon. To this day, I thank God for

His grace and mercy because He had every right to take back this golden opportunity due to the arrogance and lack of faith I displayed. Although I cannot remember exactly what the pastor said that day, I do remember that the first sentence gave me a resounding yes! Go to Abu Dhabi. Furthermore, on that day, the first of what I can only describe as *God things* started to happen after I said, yes, God, I will go.

I sat through the entire sermon and continued to hear further confirmation of God's yes. It got to a point where I thought, OK, God, I get it. You have made your point. Now, here's the crazy part. As the sermon was ending, I noticed a person sitting in the pew in front of me. Had I noticed them at any point before that moment, it would have thrown me completely off, and I surely would have missed the message and the blessing. I believe God shielded my eyes during the sermon so I would focus on Him and Him alone. God does God things.

I would like to say everything went great in Abu Dhabi after saying yes to God. I would like to be able to say this is where my chapter ends, and everything worked out happily ever after, but I cannot. Don't get me wrong. Abu Dhabi and Dubai were amazing, and everything fell into place after almost immediately submitting to God's will. I got on a plane to an unknown country with literally thirty dollars in my pocket. I had to spend what little money I had getting my passport renewed as well as getting all kinds of documents attested and sent to Abu Dhabi. Also, keep in mind that it would be thirty days before I would see my first check. But if God said go, and He knew I had thirty dollars, then I knew He would make it last thirty days. He would have to cover me many times during these thirty days, and not once did He let me down. It started at the airport when my luggage was deemed overweight, and there was a forty-five-dollar charge, which the attendant waived without me asking and before I had a chance to put on my sad puppy dog face. The blessings kept coming. Upon arrival, we were advised that our permanent housing wasn't ready yet, so we were going to stay at the Hilton. The Hilton quickly filled up, so some of us had to stay at another hotel that none of us had heard of before, so we were not happy. That was until we checked into the absolute best hotel I had ever been in. It included a free brunch buffet that I utilized to the fullest. Let's just say none of my thirty dollars had to be used for meals. Although the Hilton was very nice, it did not have a free brunch buffet. Trust me, the blessings continued. There were just too many to list, from amazing people and relationships to awesome experiences and so much more. I must, however, highlight two major blessings. About half of my family is Christian and the others are Muslim, and for most of my younger years, I was raised as a Muslim. So when the news came out that I was moving to a Muslim country, my Muslim side of the family found joy in that notion. They were still worried about me going, and most of them still objected, but being in a Muslim country was the saving grace for them. For me, it was the opposite. I was just beginning to build a relationship with my Lord and Savior, Jesus Christ, and now He was sending me to a Muslim country, where as far as I knew, Bibles were not allowed. I was pleasantly surprised to find there are many churches in the UAE, and I found one that had the presence of God unlike I had ever experienced. Everyone in the UAE is allowed to worship as they please, as long as they do not attempt to convert a Muslim to any other religion.

I said we would get back to *Yes, and…*so here we go. Unbeknownst to anyone, and I mean no one knew this, I always wanted to be a stand-up comedian. For years I would practice routines in the mirror, but because of fear and a lack of belief in myself, I never attempted to get on a stage. Aside from the training, teaching, and minor socializing with my new teacher friends, I spent the first few weeks alone most nights. Alone but not lonely. When boredom began to set in, I searched for and found a comedy class in Dubai. I signed up for it and began the weekly classes. This is where I learned the term *Yes, and…*The course was eight weeks, and during week six, we were advised that we would be performing for a live audience in two weeks as part of our graduation. I thought to myself, excuse me? I didn't see that in the syllabus. I was terrified, but I thought this must be a part of my yes to God and His yes to me.

Two weeks passed, and it was showtime. Here I was doing what I had longed to do for so many years, all because of my yes to God. Well, my performance went so well that I was invited to join the school as their newest performer, and after my very first show, I became a paid professional stand-up comedian and went on to tour the UAE for the next two years. Won't He do it? The answer is yes. So that is why *Yes, and…*. Is a major part of my life. I learned to say yes, God, and let Him handle the *and* that comes along with it.

One of the greatest gifts God gives us is choice. Some say it is as much a curse as a blessing. It is what separates us from God's other creations. A dog cannot choose to be a cat. We, however, can choose to say no, and we often do. After two years of thriving in the UAE, my teaching contract was up, and they offered to extend it. I was hitting on all cylinders. My teaching career was awesome, comedy had made me almost famous, I had met a wonderful woman who exponentially changed my life, my bank account was more than restored, and most importantly, my relationship with God was never stronger.

I turned to God again and prayed again, and His answer was just as clear as it was in that church back in New Jersey. God was not ready for me to leave. When posed with those same questions again, "Do you love me?" "Do you trust me?" My mouth said yes, but my actions said no.

I had come to the UAE because of faith and left because of fear. I rationalized in my own mind that I needed to go home because of my children, especially my daughters. They needed my protection, as if the same God that covered them for two years wouldn't continue to do so as I continued to complete the purpose He sent me to fulfill in the UAE. I was also starting to feel a little bit like I got it from here, Lord. My bank account was great, things were back on track, and I was ready to go back to the States. Actually, I really didn't want to go back, and I knew God was telling me to stay put and be still. I left anyway because I was afraid of what some people were saying about me. I was afraid of being labeled a bad father. I was even afraid of the success I was enjoying. A small part of me started to doubt if I deserved this. Even though I knew God had given it to me, because in John 10:10 ASV, it says, "I came that they may have life, and may have it abundantly."

As fast as I flourished after saying yes, God, I floundered even faster after choosing to disobey. I moved to California to be close to my daughters and began to lean on my own understanding. I felt like I would be seen as noble to give up all I had left behind in the UAE. To a certain extent, I guess it was. At least, that is what I decided my story would be. I will give you the cliff notes version of my Los Angeles experience to not belabor the point. After about a month, my bank account was emptied for the second time. The taxes for the business, which I had not been affiliated with for about five years, were not being handled properly, and my social security number was still attached to it. So once I deposited the money I had earned overseas into an American bank, it was flagged, and the IRS took every cent. I contacted them and provided proof that I had left the business years ago. They responded that they were not in the business of returning money once it was seized. They said I should pursue legal action against the other party. It was all good just a day ago. Now, without the safety net I had come back to the states with, I was once again flailing. It was one thing after another, and eventually, I ended up living in my car for about eight months.

Unlike in New Jersey, I only had one person in LA who supported me. I was much better equipped to take care of my children from halfway across the world than I was living in the same city. I do not think this was a punishment for my disobedience, but it certainly was a consequence. I share this portion of the story to contrast the difference between a yes and a no.

To be completely honest, my LA experience was far more dire than my experiences in New Jersey. I was homeless for real in LA. I had a job and managed to support my daughters, pick them up from school, make school recitals, etc. No one suspected a thing. That is what I told myself. The main difference between my New Jersey struggles and my LA struggles was that my relationship with God was strengthened so much in the UAE. I never got depressed, and I knew God was there, working things out despite the choices I made.

I mentioned God's timing earlier. He worked things out for me in His divine time. By His grace, I am once again living in my purpose according to His will, and I am again enjoying a prosperous and joyful earthly existence. I knew He would, but what I wasn't going to do was rush God to fix the mess I created. I stayed faithful, and God has given me many more chances to say yes, God! He gives you the same opportunity. What I hope you take away from what I shared is the power of saying yes, God, as well as the even Greater power of God's yes to you, which always has an and…attached to it. I love y'all.

You Can Build a Relationship with God Right Where You Are!

Troy Burgess

You can have a relationship with God regardless of where you are in your life. Building a personal relationship with God was something that I didn't understand in my youth. I was born and raised in Charleston, South Carolina. As a young man growing up in the south, my family, which included my mother, brother, and I, went to church faithfully every Sunday. Attending church weekly was the norm for me and what I had grown accustomed to. By the time I was a teenager, I had been to so many different churches I did not like going to church at all.

My mother firmly believed in the scripture, "train up a child in the way he should go, and when he is old, he will not depart from it" (Proverbs 22:6 KJV). As I got older, I discovered this scripture was interpreted in different ways. Our church would have week-long revivals, and my mother would make us attend at least three out of the five nights.

When I was young, I did not have a strong personal relationship with God. Although I knew He always had His hand on me, I didn't understand what a personal relationship with God truly entailed. I associated God with a church building rather than the Holy Spirit that lives inside of me and stays with me no matter where I go.

Accepting Christ as a teenager was not challenging for me. However, *living* for Christ was more difficult. Society is not always in alignment with the calling that God has on a believer's life. My teenage years were nowhere near perfect. And I did not dare try to carry or present myself as a disciple for the One who is perfect. In fact, I may have come off as the complete opposite, depending on who you asked. I didn't get into trouble like illegal activities, drug use, drinking, or smoking. I still felt like I did not have a heart for God. I believed in Him and feared Him, but my heart was not dedicated to representing Him. I thought that being a Christian was trying to be perfect and never doing anything wrong. Someone putting on airs like an upright individual without error. That feeling didn't feel right to me. I was trying to be something that I was not, a perfect person.

My mind was caught up in the misconceptions shown to me by others I looked up to or followed at the time. It took me getting older to realize that people don't always intentionally lead you wrong. They simply may not know a better way themselves.

As a youngster, I really enjoyed listening to different types of music, but growing up, it was presented to me that if you follow God, you had to listen only to Gospel music, which I did enjoy as well. I believed in some of the religious practices still happening today, like certain attire had to be worn in church. And if you didn't have specific "church" clothes, you shouldn't go to church. I look back now and just laugh because I was basically accepting religious practices that really had nothing to do with loving God. It seemed like I had heard more about what not to do in order to follow God than what to do. Everything from males shouldn't have their ears pierced to females must only wear full body length dresses. My revelation later in life was not to confuse man's religious practices with God's Word. Jesus said to love the Lord thy God with all your heart, soul, and mind. And to love your neighbor as yourself, and by doing so, these were the greatest of all other commandments. The older I got, the more I realized that one big hindrance to my relationship with Christ was people! I was listening to others, following what they believed to be truth, and allowing their thoughts and expectations to matter to me when it shouldn't have. The less I let people influence me, the closer I became to God. I had complicated my walk by trying to meet the expectations of others instead of asking God for His guidance and what pleased Him. I now have some great brothers and sisters in Christ, and I can turn to them about anything. I needed to receive the Word from a foundation of faith-based people, not just people trying to give me advice based on their own personal perspectives and opinions.

I had my share of obstacles in my youth, but two major circumstances really strengthened my Faith and brought me closer to God. The first was when my mother came close to being charged with a felony crime. My mother, a God-fearing woman, had a companion who made an unwise choice that affected all of our lives in ways we could not have imagined. Her companion committed a crime at her place of employment. This automatically made my mother an accomplice to the crime. Unfortunately, oftentimes in the justice system, it's not about whether you are truly guilty or not, but the appearance or perception of those in power. Eventually, my mother was given several years of probation. I thank God she was not sentenced to incarceration. My mother being freed from this ordeal was an amazing victory in my life. Not only was my mom my main level of support, but she was the closest person I knew at the time, along with my brother. I remember I was in the eleventh grade when this all happened. It was the most stressful situation I had ever gone through up to that point in my life. At the age of sixteen, I had constant thoughts about how I would take care of myself and my younger brother. I pondered obsessively on what would be done to keep a roof over our heads if the court ruling had not gone in our favor. All my prayers during these times certainly brought me closer to God in a very humbling way. The faith of so many people around us got us through this ordeal and brought me great gratitude.

Years later, at the age of twenty-two, I decided to join the US Coast Guard. I was near the end of the process of officially joining. I went to the medical screening and found that my blood pressure was elevated for some reason. I was asked a series of questions about how I felt at the time, and I replied I felt fine. I was retested, and my blood pressure was still elevated. I had to return to my home doctor and get a written note with normal pressure readings. The whole process was pending my doctor's approval. This set my entry back by six months, which at the time seemed like forever. Those months were filled with a lot of prayer and growth in my faith. These situations grew my personal relationship with God. By the time I entered the military, I had developed my own relationship with God, which worked in my favor because I needed Him for the upcoming obstacles in my life.

Although I didn't regularly attend an actual church building at the beginning of my military career, my personal relationship with Christ still grew. In fact, my first duty station was so remote that there were no places of worship anywhere near my location. However, I had a friend who became just like a brother. We strengthened each other "as iron sharpens iron" (Proverbs 27:17 NKJV). I knew that Christ was my source of being and that I could do nothing without Him. This time helped me understand that a personal relationship with God was needed in order for me to overcome any obstacle or battle. You can invite God to be with you no matter where you are in your life. The closer I got to Him, the more I realized how much I needed Him for everything. I encourage everyone to accept Christ as their personal Lord and Savior and to help others do the same. After all, eternal life is the ultimate gift.

It felt great to choose Jesus Christ for myself without being forced or made to feel guilty. It felt good to have the heart to want to do so for myself. It didn't feel out of character for me at all. I felt more joyful because I was fulfilling a calling in my life. I came to realize as I matured, I could have chosen the Lord no matter where I was or what I was doing in my life, as long as it was with a genuine heart. This applies to everyone, whether you are in politics, construction, the service industry, etc. It even applies to you if you are doing something illegal or unethical. We all need to call on Him, and He will meet us exactly where we are. A personal relationship is just that, personal. And while testimonies need to be shared, they are not a replacement for your own personal relationship with Christ. Your relationship is not based on another's judgment or opinion. I believe opinions can hinder folks from coming to God wholeheartedly. Many people think along the lines of, well, I've done this, I've done that, and what will people who know me think or say? It's honestly not their place.

Christ was in me, but the choice needed to be made to remain in Him. In 2008, I heard a life-changing sermon by a pastor in the Maryland area where I was stationed. For most of my life, the only Bible translation I knew was the King James Version. I rarely read the Bible in context because I didn't grasp the King James Version, which was written in Old English text. At the age of thirty-one, I told my mother about my challenges with understanding biblical verses clearly, and she purchased a life application study Bible as a gift for me. I have always loved to read and enjoyed the knowledge that came from reading. I read that Bible from front to back, word for word, and highlighted it throughout. It took me a little over a year, but I did complete it! Ironically, when my wife and I met, we were both reading the very same Bible and were almost in the exact same location with our reading. It was life-changing to have read the Word of God for myself. I was finally at a point where if I heard something that didn't line up with the Word, I knew that it was not of God.

Reading the Word for myself and understanding it was a major revelation in my relationship with God. I now know the Word for myself and no longer need to take someone else's word for it. Much of what I had been taught about the Word of God did not line up with the actual Word of God at all. It was the repetitive and constant conditioning that caused me to believe the wrong things about God and His Word. The reading I did gave me peace and a new connection with God that I never had previously experienced. I went through my Bible highlights and read the breakdown of the scriptures, and it made sense to me in a very different light. I had learned not to be concerned with fitting the mold or being what society said I should be as a Christian. I started focusing on what God needed me to be for Him. I started leading by example with the gifts that He has given to me. Jesus Christ is the greatest example who ever lived. His methods led with love. His strength was His love. He is love. Unfortunately, love is not the most respected quality in men these days and is often viewed as a sign of weakness. That must change because of the greatest example set by the greatest man to ever walk this earth.

I have always been an easygoing individual, but early in my youth, I could be very cold-hearted. I took things personally and didn't want my kindness taken for weakness. It was not until God brought me to a certain point in my life that I realized much of what I had learned from society was nonsense. These beliefs led me on a road to nowhere. I began to understand that being a man had nothing to do with being tough. In today's world, people are often hurt because of silly disputes that can be easily resolved, but there's always a party that must prove themselves to friends or others who do not have their best interest at heart. These types of actions without thinking things through are commonly praised and glorified in our society and can be very influential to a young, impressionable mind. This way of thinking is foolish. I'm not saying that you should not stand up for yourself but having God-Given discernment will provide you the guidance to handle your situation with wisdom.

I have seen tests arise and come from anywhere. You can be having the best day until someone in traffic, at a store, in the neighborhood, or at work does or says something that can send you over the edge. It's in those moments you have to learn to make a choice. You can either have the heart to ask God for His guidance or just react negatively in your flesh. Just know that once you give in to your flesh, you no longer have control over what you'll say or do. Being able to speak kind words after someone curses at you takes the love of God. There have been times when I have passed the test of love and other times when I have failed it miserably. I know my walk with God is a daily choice I must make. And I am grateful that He will never leave my side nor forsake me.

Going to church was one thing, but getting connected to the people in the Kingdom was something completely different for me. I had no idea what any of my spiritual gifts were or how to use them. As a child, I was an usher, but that was basically because it was a requirement in the youth program I attended. Early on, I was able to see some of the inner workings of how the spirit of confusion could creep into a church, turn it upside down, and cause a horrible mess. Confusion was never my style. As I got older, I found myself doing the opposite of what I did in my youth. My mom would always have us sit in the front during service. Once I began to go to church on my own, I sat in the very back and then left right after the service was over while others hung around and chit-chatted.

What I discovered about myself is that I enjoyed the small interactive groups more than the larger ones. The groups that met during the week either at someone's home, a park, a coffee shop, or anywhere five to ten people could fellowship and just be themselves. I remember when I signed up for the prison ministry. It was at a standstill, though, so nothing ever came of it. Next, I partnered with some men for a youth mentoring program on Saturday evenings, and I enjoyed it. Through the church, I was eventually led to coach youth sports, and I loved it! Breaking out into these smaller groups allowed me to get to know people, and they began to open themselves up to me and share their experiences with me.

I met people who struggled with the size of their place of worship, the congregation was so large that they never felt connected. Others told me that they were trying to connect but felt that they were not accepted because either they weren't married, had kids out of wedlock, or provided any number of other ridiculous reasons. These experiences confirmed what I had always felt in my heart, that it was hard for people to truly open up for fear of being judged. People can be very cliquish. It isn't always a bad thing since most of us like to be around like-minded individuals or someone with whom we can easily connect. It's when others feel shunned or excluded that it becomes an issue. In all of my experiences with places of worship, most do a fantastic job at having events and gatherings where people can come together and connect. A member of one of the small life groups I attended was used by God to give me the opportunity to meet my wife.

This member bought me a ticket to support a non-profit fundraiser that I had no intention of attending. In fact, a good friend had invited me to a boxing match in Atlantic City that very same night. If someone purchases a ticket for me to an event, I am not the type to not show up, even though I didn't ask them to purchase the ticket. I always strive to do things with a certain level of decency. So I went to the fundraising event, not really in the best of moods. And lo and behold, God had a reason for me to be there. God knew I would be meeting my lifelong partner at this event.

Today, I am a proud member and co-founder of a faith-based, non-profit organization called Hope at the Cross. This is a group of Brothers who have all come together through the vision of our leader to do work for Christ by reaching out and helping youth and their families who have been impacted by traumatic events and experiences. God had a place for me this whole time, but I needed to keep the faith to receive it. Things were slowly revealed to me over time and did not happen overnight.

There's a place for all of us in God's Kingdom. Some may be called to be around hundreds of people, while others may be called to smaller groups or not many people at all. Begin where you are, just you and God. I recommend getting an easy-to-read Bible that you can understand and that you enjoy reading. Growing up, the pastor would tell the congregation to turn to a scripture. I would grab the Bible in the front pew and try to turn to the scripture. But, by the time I found it, if I found it at all, the reading was over. One day, at a different church, the Pastor told the congregation to use the table of contents, lol, because that's what it was there for. You see, there is no need to be a hero or try to prove that you know something you are not familiar with. Don't feel like you have to wait until you get your life together to find God and say yes to God. Contrary to public opinion, coming to Christ is not only for people who think they are better than others, goodie two shoes, or even Bible thumpers. Christ is for the hurting, the sick, the messed up, the down on your luck, the world turned upside down people who are considered a hot mess. The real truth of the matter is that we are *all* a work in progress, regardless of what we *think* about one another.

If you had a bad experience with your first, or prior, introduction to God, and it was due to someone else, then I encourage you to go to God and have a relationship for yourself. God will surround you with the right supporting cast in your life. Just because you trust someone and they may even be like family to you, it doesn't make their words or advice biblical truth. Get God's Word for yourself. You do not have to receive any negativity spoken into or over your life. Your value is not based on other people's thoughts of you. Your value won't be found with your next boyfriend, girlfriend, or spouse. Other people are not what you need to be made whole. You need, I need, we all need Christ's *love*. So reach out to Him right now, wherever you are, and tell Him yes!

God Opened a Door for Me

Rodney Peake

You are my hiding place; You preserve me from trouble; You surround me with songs of deliverance. Selah (Psalm 32:7 NASB1995).

With no father in my life, I know that God kept me. I would have been on a much different path had it not been for the grace of God! My mother worked overnight while raising a son in the city of East Orange, right on the border of Newark, New Jersey. I often hear my mother's words as if it was yesterday, "Thank you, son, for never giving me trouble." Right after she said it, I immediately had to turn to God and say thank you for keeping me.

I thank God for giving me the discernment growing up to realize when my friends were going too far and for allowing me to see that jail wasn't the answer for me. Not only was it not the answer for me, but it would have broken my mother's heart. The sacrifices she made for me were monumental. She worked overnight to support me, and eventually, when she changed shifts, she had to catch a bus when it was still dark outside at five o'clock in the morning and ride thirty miles to work.

My mother's hard work found its way into my employment DNA. She worked hard, and so I learned my work ethic from my mom. My mom also made sacrifices, like keeping her dating life away from me. She never left me alone with a boyfriend. God only knows what could have happened. I thank God for giving me a mother's love. A mother's love is the closest thing to God's love that we have on this earth. So I implore anyone to always cherish a mother's love because when it's gone, you can't get it back.

THE BEGINNING

My journey in this life has been like a ride on a roller coaster. The very first time I said yes to God was as a nine-year-old when I accepted Christ as my Lord and Savior. From age nine until twelve, I felt like I was on fire! Then, things took a turn and I started to backslide. During this time, I had fist fights, alcohol binges, and a time or two indulging in marijuana. The only thing that saved me from smoking it more was the lack of control it left me feeling. I thought to myself how I didn't want this lack of control to hinder my fighting ability if someone that didn't like me wanted to fight!

One of my biggest struggles early on was growing up without a father. My mother was a great mom. However, it takes a man to raise a son to be a man. I had reached the age where I wanted a girlfriend, and as an awkward teenager with no father in my life to teach me, I had no idea how to get one. Like others in my situation, there were so many tools missing from my manhood toolbox that I felt like I was starting behind the eight ball. There was no father to teach me how to pick up girls, no father to teach me how to play sports, no father to advocate on my behalf for not being given a fair shot at playing sports, and no father to tell me the things a man should be responsible for in a marriage.

In short, as I got older, I believed I was half the man I could have been without a good father in my life. It may be easy for some to say that this can't be true, but for Rodney Peake, it is my truth. For most of my early adult life, I stumbled my way through making manly decisions, starting with my ability to manage bills and my credit. I also struggled with not keeping my word. Too many times, I would say I was going to do something and not do it! When I was a kid, we wanted to be cool, so we would say, "word is bond." However, we did not fully understand what we were saying. Your word truly is your bond, and you need to stay true to what you say.

At the beginning of our marriage, as a husband, I allowed my wife to lead us. What to do, when to do it, and how to do it. When it came to purchasing our first, second, and third houses, in a real but joking manner, I would say to her, "What did you get me into?" When God began to change the dynamic of our relationship, I had to learn God's true design for marriage. I needed to know that the husband gets his instructions from God, and his wife follows the instructions God has given to her husband.

As a young man in my twenties and early thirties, my confidence was severely shaken because I struggled with abandonment due to my father leaving. I developed what a marriage counselor once told me was conflict avoidance. I would avoid conflict of any kind and at all costs. From telling people what they wanted to hear to creating elaborate lies at times, my confidence was so fractured that I would point out any flaw I noticed in someone else just to cover up my own flaws. This behavior caused me to believe there was no way God could ever use someone like me! Never mind that He used a drunk (Noah), a murderer (Paul), an adulterer (David), and a liar (Abraham). I thought the stuff in my mind was far worse. Just think, which I didn't, in spite of all my junk, He still died on the cross for me and you! And Noah, Paul, David, and Abraham.

MY DISRUPTED LIFE

When my wife and I were first married, my mother got breast cancer. She had to undergo surgery to remove a lump from her breast. I was right there when she woke up from surgery. At every turn, she had always been there for me, so it was unquestionable that I would be there for her. During her recovery, my mom stayed with my wife and me. She made a full recovery, or so we thought. It was ten years later that her terrible doctors in New Jersey had her thinking she was suffering from bad arthritis. As it turned out, the cancer had metastasized. We immediately moved her to Maryland to be treated at Johns Hopkins Hospital. When I stop and reflect back on it, it was such an incredible sacrifice on my wife's part that I know God gave me a gift in my wife. A gift that I often took for granted.

I immediately changed my shift to work nights so I could take my mom to chemo and be present for her doctor's appointments. I tried to make sure I did everything I could to make things easy for mom and her doctor's visits. After two years of chemotherapy treatments, my mom succumbed to cancer. As always, I was right by her side until the very end. People usually say they wish they could be by their loved one's side in their final moments. Being by her side was one of the most difficult things I have ever been through. The only thing that got me through it, and calmed her down, was the Word of God. Once, while my mom was in hospice, I had gone home to rest. My cousin, who had stayed behind, called me, and I could hear my mother screaming in the background, "Hardy! Hardy!" My family probably believes that she was calling out to her brother. His name was Harden Rout, but his nickname was Hardy. This is not true! Since I was a little boy, and up until the day she passed, she would call me Hardy, especially whenever she got excited or was panicking. She would do it so much that I would often ask her why she didn't just name me Hardy. She would laugh and say, "I should have." When I returned to the hospital, she was staring at each corner of the room, panicked. My wife had the wherewithal to ask everyone to leave me alone with my mother. After everyone left, I picked up the Bible and read the entire book of Psalms to her. My mother immediately calmed down, and there was a sense of peace that filled the room until she took her last breath. As I write this, I can't hold back the tears. It even took years before I could ride through Baltimore without thinking about Pauline Peake. To this day, I still think about her when I ride past Johns Hopkins Hospital.

Even though I did everything I could in those last two years, I still struggled with guilt. I struggled with one incident in particular. I was the one who took my mother to every chemo treatment and sat with her at every doctor's appointment, asking every question possible. One day after chemo, my mother wanted to go back to our favorite place to get a crab cake sandwich. But because I was running late for work (if I could, I would put an angry emoji here), I said no. That *no* haunted me for *years*. It took much prayer before I finally was able to reconcile it with God and myself. I loved God, but at that time, I couldn't understand His Will. Although my mom's soul was secure, I couldn't understand why He would take her from me and shatter my world. I sit here writing this at fifty-five years of life. The very same age my mother was when she passed and my life was disrupted!

PERMISSIVE RUNNING

I can still remember it like it was yesterday when I received the second call from God for my life. The first call was accepting Christ. It was in my shower, of all places. It was there I heard the voice of God. I wish I could say it was the most awesome and great experience. The truth is, God's voice scared the daylights out of me! I was truly naked and afraid! I hurried out of the shower, saying to myself, "God doesn't want me to preach. Not the quiet, shy guy that spent so much time using his fists as a security blanket instead of using his words! Not the guy who had conflict avoidance issues, who would lie his way out of situations." I called the chairman of our deacon board and told him in a panic, "I heard the voice of God and I need to be a Deacon!" Notice the 'I.' He actually had to slow me down. He encouraged me to get into a Bible study and to serve on a ministry. After getting into Bible Study and serving on a few different ministries faithfully, I was selected by my pastor to walk in a leadership role with about fifteen other men. After about two months of training, the group was narrowed down to seven men. One day in a meeting, the pastor asked the group what role each of us believed we were called to by God. My wife, who was privy to everything that had taken place, sat confused when it came to my time to answer and I didn't say "deacon" as the others did. One by one, they all said, "I believe I'm called to the office of deacon." I, however, said, "I don't know." It was either that or say what I heard in the shower. And I had absolutely no intention of doing that. I didn't even believe it myself. How could I tell the woman I had not been living with understanding, that I heard God calling me to preach? Eventually, I told her it was because I didn't hear God call me to deacon. I chose deacon because I thought I must have misunderstood God.

The truth is, I have so many fears and thoughts that don't seem to be conducive to being a preacher, like… What if I hear crickets? What if I ramble on incoherently? What if I don't sound like my pastor, or better yet, my grandfather, the late Reverend John Henry Rout? What if I'm faced with conflict, or what if I have to lie my way out of something? So I convinced myself God wouldn't be calling me to preach His Word! And so, I settled into being a deacon! The truth is that I have not been the ideal deacon. My house was not in order., Remember, I was not living with my wife with understanding. My daughters were struggling with respect, and I needed to do a better job of looking after my family group. My tithing needed to improve. I would often pay bills first. I was very good at praying by myself too, but not good at praying with my wife. In addition, I had some misplaced anger issues with her.

THE TUGS

I served as a deacon for three years before I got what I call my first tug. It came in the form of a major stroke. The year I had my major stroke, two celebrities died from the same type of stroke. I, on the other hand, was spared by God. I was sitting in a Peruvian chicken restaurant, and the world started spinning. I looked at the table beside me, and a gentleman was sitting there, but my pride kept me from asking him for help. I eventually stumbled into a single-use bathroom and locked the door behind me. I threw up, sat on the edge of the toilet, and all I could do was look up and say to God, "not on the toilet, Lord." I was able to muster up the strength to stumble back out of the restroom, slide down the wall and call out for help. There was a nurse that was in the restaurant who came to my aid, and she immediately sprang into action. She knew everything to do. Think about it. I got up out of a single-use bathroom and there just happened to be a nurse in the restaurant at the same time. The really interesting thing was that the major part of my stroke did not happen in the restaurant. It happened in the emergency room, right in front of a team of doctors that just so happened to be making their rounds. To quote a line I heard from a sermon, "Nothing just happens!"

    I initially lost, and eventually regained, feeling on my left side. By the time I went into therapy, I was able to walk with a cane. The first minutes of my first session were done with a walker. My therapist thought I would do well with a cane, and much to the dismay of everyone in there, including me, it worked. I had no explanation but God. During my time in the hospital and in-patient therapy, I would tell anyone who came to visit me I didn't know why God saved me. In fact, He not only saved me, but He gave me 95 percent of my movements and strength back! Most people who see me are amazed that I suffered a major stroke. However, pretending not to hear the call on my life, I still settled right back into being a deacon. All was not well. I was still at war in my home and with myself. And by not surrendering fully to God, I was at war with God!

The second tug came in the form of the dreaded big C for cancer. Following my stroke, I visited a number of doctors, and they determined that I needed to keep an eye on my prostate numbers. After a few years, I was diagnosed with prostate cancer. I actually was not shaken by the diagnosis because of my faith in God. I was shaken by the thought of having to be put under anesthesia. I was frightened by the dreams that awaited me while I was under. I was so frightened by it that I refused any type of anesthesia during the biopsy. What a big mistake. The funny thing is, it turns out that the anesthesia was the best sleep I had in twenty years. You would think by now I would wake up and listen to God. Not me. I settled right back into being a deacon again.

The final tug was when I eventually tore my rotator cuff after years of carrying heavy ladders. I was facing retirement after my fifty-fifth birthday and a twenty-four-year career as a technician. In the meantime, my pastor assigned some of the men of the church to speak on a Good Friday, and wouldn't you know it, Mr. running man was one of the men who spoke, actually preached. It was during that assignment that I finally had enough of running and pretending. I called my pastor and informed him that I was tired of running and decided to say yes to God to preach His Word!

WHEN GOD CLOSES ONE DOOR, HE OPENS ANOTHER

When God closes one door, He opens another. This is said so much in church that, as Christians, I think some of us have lost sight of what it actually means. There I was, with a torn rotator cuff and 95 percent mobility. The 5 percent I was missing was getting on and off of the floor, which was part of my job. I was facing certain retirement because of it. I was on light duty with the expectation of needing surgery on my rotator cuff. The pain was so great that I would have to take Advil just to get me through the day. I had finally said yes to God to preach His Word! I was given another assignment to preach a Wednesday night service. I put the time in. I studied and allowed God to help me deal with my fears about preaching. My wife, who had already been a minister for several years, encouraged me by saying that if I studied God's Word and preached His message, I would be prepared. She also helped me by sharing resources and tools she had used.

A conversation with my Aunt Gloria encouraged me more than she knew. She was my mother's sister and the daughter of the man on earth that I admired the most, my grandfather, the late Reverend John Henry Rout. He was a pastor, a leader, a teacher, and a carpenter. He mentored and raised up the pastors of four churches that he had built. He also built his house attached to the final church. I even helped dig the foundation of the formal living room my Grandmother asked him to build. I didn't last past the foundation, but that's a story for a different book. When I say built, I mean physically built!

My Aunt Gloria shared with me my grandfather's fears, wishes, hopes, and dreams for his family. She told me that I would be a better preacher than he was. She filled me with so much confidence it was apparent God had made her talk to me! Soon after that conversation, I was given another assignment to preach the Wednesday night service again. Slowly, my somewhat juvenile fears started to wither away. Get back, Satan. You have no place here!

It was June 25, a little more than a month from my birthday and my looming forced retirement. I received a call out of the blue. God was at work again. The call was about an offer for a position in my company's engineering department. Initially, I was apprehensive. I had been a technician for twenty-four years, and I wasn't sure

I could cut it in the engineering department. The position came with the ability to work from home. Since gas prices had reached an all-time high, this sounded like a great offer, to say the least.

Needless to say, I took the offer! I met my new supervisor, and the meeting went so well, it was like God was saying, "I got you!" During this new transition, I was trained by one of the best trainers I'd had in forty years of being in the workforce. To top it all off, God had begun to heal the relationship with my family! Where my wife and I had been at war with one another, God began to work. We actually were assigned to help on the mission field in the area of marriage. We were also asked to write a chapter in a book about marriage!

I said yes to God, and as He promised in 2 Chronicles 7:14 (NKJV), "if My people who are called by My name will humble themselves, and pray and seek My face, and turn from their wicked ways, then I will hear from heaven, and will forgive their sin and heal their land." He once again forgave me of my sins, and He healed my land! My life is far less of a roller coaster ride and becoming more and more stable. Even though I was foolish and took my time, all I can say is thank you, Jesus, for always being a loving and patient God. I still say, "yes, God.

About the Authors

Dominique Clark is a devoted husband and a loving father. He is a man who acknowledges God in all his ways and uses his platform to show God's grace and mercy in his life as well as in the lives of others. The youngest of seven children, Dominique attended Prince Georges County public schools and grew up in a home that was built on Christian belief.

Dominique accepted Jesus Christ as his Lord and Savior in 2012 and was baptized in 2015. In his journey, Dominique discovered that there is genetic pain that has been passed down to him and he seeks to break the generational curses without blaming others.

Dominique is involved in men's spiritual accountability groups and a men's prayer call at his church. Most of all, Dominique hopes to help others by telling his story of when he finally said yes to God's will for his life.

Anthony Proctor has a heart for God, his family, and the community. Tony was born in Washington, DC, and was raised in New York City, where he learned how to be street savvy. He has a bachelor's degree in psychology and is a Certified Peer Recovery Specialist, helping returning citizens make their transition from prison back into society.

He retired as a letter carrier and union representative from the US Postal Service. Tony and his brother and sister were raised by their mother. Going through life's challenges, he received custody of his daughter. God later blessed Tony with a beautiful wife who had two children. They now have five grandchildren. Tony and his wife serve nationally and internationally in God's Kingdom. Tony has been set aside as a pastor and is now a God Chaser! His life verse is "Trust in the Lord with all your Heart" (Proverbs 3:5 NKJV).

About the Authors

Harold Ferrell, a native of Syracuse, New York, has called Prince Georges County, Maryland, home for more than thirty years. He is a Senior Travel Consultant with one of the country's leading travel management companies. He is both excited and honored to be a part of this "Yes, God" project.

One of his favorite scriptures is Ephesians 3:20 (NKJV), "Now to Him who is able to do exceedingly abundantly above all that we ask or think, according to the power that works in us." He enjoys performing in his church's drama ministry. He is an avid sports fan and loves traveling, photography, and fishing. Harold and his wife have three adult children; one is deceased.

To connect, email him at
hjferrell@hotmail.com

Grayling V.G. Sterling Sr. is the oldest of six children. He is a God-fearing man who loves the Lord and constantly strives to be obedient to His will. Grayling is an entrepreneur, a business owner, and a retired veteran who served in the Marines for eight years and in the Army for fifteen years. He is a War Veteran of Dessert Shield/Storm. He has served as Chairman of the Board of Trustees at Mt. Calvary Baptist Church of Lanham, where he has been part of several ministries.

Grayling has a spirit of service and loves helping others. He has been a mentor to youth as well as adults and gives of his time freely. He loves fishing and working with his hands, whether repairing or building things. He stays busy.

Grayling is married and has three sons and a grandson. Grayling is currently enjoying retirement life with his wife, Cheryl.

About the Authors

Andre Reynolds is a teacher, speaker, and stand-up comedian with a passion for serving others. A native of Newark, New Jersey, he has always advocated for the special needs community, the unhoused, and at-risk women.

Andre is a gifted communicator with a bachelor's degree in communications from Rutgers University. Andre obtained his teaching certification in early childhood education from Montclair University.

Having lived in multiple countries, Andre is an international educator and entertainer. He is affectionately known as "Mr. Andre" to his students and his audiences. He puts God first in all of his endeavors and is certain that saying "yes" to God has given his life purpose and joy. Andre believes that we are all on earth to serve God and God's people.

> To connect, email him at
> reynoldsatr@gmail.com

Troy Burgess was born and raised by his mother in North Charleston, SC. He is a loving Father who cherishes spending time with his wife and children. In his free time, Troy enjoys reading books, playing chess, and watching sports.

He attended Gordon H. Garrett Academy of Technology High School and served in the US Coast Guard for over twenty years. Troy has traveled throughout the world assisting in Military search and rescue missions, as well as response missions.

He and his wife share two children, ages seven and three. Troy has received humanitarian awards from the city for helping and assisting others. His mission is to help others grow and see a positive way of life.

Troy is a proud member of Hope at the Cross, a non-profit organization dedicated to helping youth impacted by traumatic events. Troy currently resides with his family in Anne Arundel County, Maryland.

About the Authors

Rodney Peake is a gifted writer and director. He has written eight successful stage plays and a number of skits. He is also a best-selling author of two books on marriage and is currently working on his next book project and stage play.

Rodney is a new minister at Mt Calvary Baptist Church of Lanham, under Bishop Charles E. Cato, Sr. He currently works for a major telecommunications company as a Facilities Assistant in the Engineering department.

He has won several Public Speaking Awards with Toastmasters International and is looking forward to what God has for him in this next season of his life.

Rodney is a father of two daughters, Zarina and Nia, and the husband of Michele Noel-Peake, his high school sweetheart. Rodney's life verse is 1 John 5:12-15.

**For group or individual coaching or
to book a speaking engagement,
contact minister and life coach Michele at:**

**www.michelereneeconsulting.com
On Facebook @ Michele Renee Consulting
On Instagram @ MinisterMichele
On YouTube @ Michele Renee Consulting**

CREATING DISTINCTIVE BOOKS WITH INTENTIONAL RESULTS

We're a collaborative group of creative masterminds with a mission to produce high-quality books to position you for monumental success in the marketplace.

Our professional team of writers, editors, designers, and marketing strategists work closely together to ensure that every detail of your book is a clear representation of the message in your writing.

Want to know more?
Write to us at info@publishyourgift.com
or call (888) 949-6228

Discover great books, exclusive offers, and more at
www.PublishYourGift.com

Connect with us on social media

@publishyourgift

www.ingramcontent.com/pod-product-compliance
Lightning Source LLC
Chambersburg PA
CBHW071902070526
44583CB00016B/1813